IF I KNEW
THEN
WHAT I KNOW
NOW

YOUTH WORKERS SHARE
THEIR WORST FAILURES
AND BEST ADVICE

LEN WOODS & DAVE VEERMAN

IF I KNEW
THEN
WHAT I KNOW
NOW

YOUTH WORKERS SHARE
THEIR WORST FAILURES
AND BEST ADVICE

LEN WOODS &
DAVE VEERMAN

ZONDERVAN®

ZONDERVAN.com/
AUTHORTRACKER
follow your favorite authors

youth
specialties

YOUTH SPECIALTIES

If I Knew Then What I Know Now
Copyright 2009 by The Livingstone Corporation

Youth Specialties resources, 1890 Cordell Ct. Ste. 105, El Cajon, CA 92020 are published by Zondervan, 5300 Patterson Ave. SE, Grand Rapids, MI 49530.

ISBN 978-0-310-28602-8

Produced with the assistance of The Livingstone Corporation
Cover design by David Conn
Cover image by © Image Source/Corbis
Interior design by Brandi Etheredge Design

Printed in the United States of America

09 10 11 12 13 14 15 • 20 19 18 17 16 15 14 13 12 11 10 9 8 7 6 5 4 3 2 1

CONTENTS

FIRST THINGS FIRST

One of my (Len) favorite cartoons is set in ancient China. Five men in traditional garb stand in a circle amidst a vast landscape of rolling hills. One is speaking. The caption reads: "Gentlemen, we have a heck of a wall to build. I suggest we get started."

How odd to consider that there was a day when the 4,000-mile-long Great Wall of China didn't exist. Not a single brick was in place.

Then someone got an idea. Maybe a lot of soul searching and consultation followed. There were discussions. Debates. Then a decision: *Let's do it!*

Explicit plans were made. A team of workers was gathered, motivated, and led. *Centuries* of backbreaking construction followed.

The eventual result? An architectural and cultural marvel. One of the acknowledged wonders of the world.

Enduring, successful youth ministries are built the same way—good ideas (or, more accurately, "God ideas"!) are hashed out, refined, and implemented by gifted people through much wise planning and hard work. But if we're not asking the right questions from the very beginning, then our efforts to build a thriving and God-honoring student ministry can crumble.

Between us, the two authors of this book have spent nearly 60 years working in the field of youth ministry. And *If I Knew Then What I Know Now* is our attempt to share some of the hard lessons we've learned from experience. We've asked ourselves what we wish we'd known from the very beginning, and we've also asked dozens of other seasoned youth ministry veterans to share their responses to the same question. The result is the book you now hold in your hands.

One of the most essential truths we've learned is that you can't reach out to teenagers if your own house isn't in order. If we knew then what we know now, then instead of immediately diving into a frenetic ministry schedule from Day 1, we would have taken the time to ask ourselves five hugely important questions:

- Is my spiritual foundation solid?
- What are my motives?
- What exactly is the mission?
- What is my plan?
- What are my expectations?

These are great questions for you to ask as well.

IS MY SPIRITUAL FOUNDATION SOLID?

Chris Larsen grew up in what he calls a "vaguely religious home." His father was an agnostic Mormon, and his mother was an apathetic Baptist. Because Chris' mom still believed in God, the family would attend the Baptist church whenever guilt overrode his mom's weekend sleep patterns. Chris explains,

> I learned early on the importance of the closing "invitation." I noticed how people were celebrated when they "walked the aisle"—especially on that last verse where God finally moved strong enough on the heart of some white-knuckled pew-grabber.
>
> I remember the day—at about the age of 10—when I got to be that celebrated kid. When my friend left the pew, I quickly followed, afraid to be left alone in the back row. When I got down front, the pastor asked me what I wanted to do. I shrugged, since I'd never been down front before. He guided me through a prayer. Then I filled out an information card with the help of a well-meaning blue-haired lady. On the spot, I was introduced to the congregation, and I shook what seemed like a thousand hands of smiling well-wishers. I was baptized that same night.

For the next several years, anytime Chris would talk to anyone about faith or being a Christian, he'd refer back to that experience where he fulfilled his spiritual obligations to God and the watching congregation. He was in high school before anyone in the church seemed to care about more than his conversion story. Chris recalls,

> I was in Houston at the time, and a youth minister named Johnny Brady began the seemingly impossible task of investing in me as an individual and not a job requirement. He asked about my family and invited me to his home. He spent a lot of time with me and continued pursuing me even when I avoided him. I rebelled against everything he taught me. And even though I had no place for religion or God in my life, Johnny was one of the few people I trusted.

After high school graduation, Chris went into the military. During a Christmas leave, Johnny invited Chris to be a chaperone on the youth midwinter retreat. That was a significant weekend for Chris because he realized how much he'd neglected the spiritual dimension of his life, and he decided to get involved in church when he got off leave. He began actively checking out nearby churches, depending upon the girl he was dating at the time.

Eventually Chris was stationed in the Houston area near his home church. He got involved again, volunteered with the youth ministry, and became a leader. When the youth minister asked Chris to teach the seventh-grade boys Sunday school class, he did it and loved it. A while later he was asked to be the middle school director and then the youth ministry associate. Chris began to feel as though ministry might be what he was supposed to do. So because of his good standing in the church and his 10-year-old aisle-walk story, he was licensed to ministry.

That July the church held a good old-fashioned revival. As the youth associate, Chris was responsible for organizing the youth pizza-pack-a-pew night. Chris describes the experience:

> After dinner, we bait-and-switched these pepperoni-stuffed students into the worship center so the guest evangelist could give them the food their souls craved. I was in the second row, and the preacher talked about all the things people use to claim a relationship with God. He said some assume church membership is a means to grace. Others believe they are right with God because they've served enough or taught a Sunday school class. Still others feel as though they will gain access to heaven because they are "in ministry."
>
> One by one, this traveling evangelist took away all the religious credentials I assumed made me right with God. And I realized that night that a relationship with God was by grace, through faith, and not the product of walking an aisle or participating in religious activities.
>
> During the invitation, I took the youth minister up to the altar. He thought we were going up front to pray for some poor, lost kid—or perhaps for some poor, lost deacon. I told him I wasn't a Christian. He sat there momentarily with a stunned look on his face.
>
> "What?" he stammered.
>
> "I'm not a Christian," I said.
>
> He sat for a moment, and then he turned to me and said, "Well, you know what to do."
>
> So, as I tell the story, I led myself to Christ. Not exactly, but in those moments I consciously put my trust in him. I stopped relying on anything righteous I had done (walking an aisle) or anything I was doing

(working with kids and so forth) and simply trusted in what Christ had done for me.

How great, at last, to really know the God I'd been so busy trying to introduce teenagers to!

Discussion Questions

1. When did you, in the words of John 1:12, "receive Christ" and become a child of God?

2. Frederick Buechner wrote, "Doubts are the ants in the pants of faith... they keep it awake and moving." In other words, it's not wrong to have occasional doubts. But why is persistent doubt about one's spiritual condition a serious matter?

3. Why is it dangerous to gauge our spiritual position (or condition) based on feelings?

4. Some people say that expressing or espousing spiritual certainty is arrogant or foolish. Do you agree or disagree? Why?

For Further Study

• Spend some time reflecting on Ephesians 2:8-9. According to this passage, is spiritual salvation a gracious gift or is it something we work for?

• Meditate on 1 John 5:11-13.

Avoiding an Avoidable Mess

• If you aren't sure you know Christ in a personal way, make an appointment with a respected Christian leader. Better to suffer a bruised ego than to launch into ministry with an empty or darkened heart.

• If discussing your doubts is too intimidating or embarrassing, then see if this prayer reflects the desire of your heart:

God, if I'm honest, I'm not real sure where I stand in relation to you. I have various doubts and uncertainties. But I want to know you. I want to be right with you. I do believe Jesus died to pay for my sins. I do believe he rose from the dead and that he offers forgiveness and life to all who put their faith in him. I want to do that right now. I believe Jesus is my only hope. I'm not trusting in anything or anyone else. My faith is in Christ. I want the eternal life, the new life you offer. Thank you for loving me and sending Christ to die for me. Now, God, as your child by faith, help me to live for you. By the power of your Holy Spirit, help me become the person you created me to be.

WHAT ARE MY *MOTIVES*?

How does somebody end up in ministry, much less *youth* ministry, of all things? Why work with teenagers when you could be an investment banker or a ski instructor—or maybe an investment banker who *marries* a (gorgeous) ski instructor?

Or, if you're into volunteerism, why not give a few hours each month to a prestigious foundation? Become a tour guide at a museum? At least in those settings you could network and pad the old résumé. Why would people in their right minds choose—knowingly, willingly—to work with youth? Maybe your story parallels—at least in part—my own.

As a student at LSU, I (Len) had long anticipated participating in a summer mission trip to Europe after my junior year. When that door slammed shut unexpectedly at the last minute, I was stunned: I'd been pretty certain God had called me to minister to all those French and Italian women who needed the gospel (and possibly a handful of European guys, too). Suddenly, I was at a loss.

It was mid-April—much too late to apply for a journalism internship. And in a city with almost 40,000 college students, even minimum-wage job openings were rare.

I prayed. Asked around. Perused the classified ads. Made some phone calls. Nothing.

Then out of the blue, I heard about a church in the New Orleans suburbs that was looking to hire a couple of college students as summer interns to work with junior high students.

With nothing to lose—and no other prospects on the horizon—I interviewed. What were my three "credentials"?

- I was a Christian seeking to walk with God (with some basic Campus Crusade training).
- I was experienced; that is, I'd somehow survived grades six through eight mostly intact—no small feat.
- I was eager. I really needed *something*—something meaningful to do and something that would help me pay my bills.

When the church offered the position, I wondered briefly about Groucho Marx's famous quip: "I don't want to belong to any club that would accept me as a member." But with my portion of the rent due ($133.33), I snapped up the offer.

It ended up being a great summer. Actually, it was fantastic. Trips, crazy youth meetings, serious Bible studies, informal times spent hanging out with kids, outreaches. I confess I had no clue what I was doing most of the time. But each day I felt *used*—in the best possible way. At bedtime each night, I felt *spent*—but it was a good kind of tired. I had low moments to be sure. There were a few jerky, unresponsive kids. And some decisions and actions I regretted. Still, I'd never felt such day-to-day *joy*. I guess what I mostly felt was *alive*.

As my fast-paced summer internship drew to a close, I began to dread my final year of college. I began to ponder *What now?*

Malcolm Muggeridge, the British journalist who became a Christian after a long life of skepticism, once said, "Every happening, great and small, is a parable whereby God speaks to us, and the art of life is to get the message." That's what I was wrestling with as I returned to school. Was there some sort of divine message for me in my summer youth experience? Was God guiding me? In my joy and fulfillment was God whispering to me, "Yes, Len, walk this way. Do *this* thing—work with youth"?

"Why?" is a question that every fledgling youth pastor or would-be youth worker needs to ask herself. *Why am I considering working with teens? Does youth ministry fit the way I'm wired? Is this a God-directed thing? Is God calling me? Guiding me? Wooing me? Pushing or pulling me? Or is this venture into youth ministry something of my own doing, something I've concocted and orchestrated? Do I want to work with youth for the right reasons—or for all the wrong reasons?*

I still have questions as I look back on my own story. Did I seek out youth ministry or did

BAD REASONS FOR DOING YOUTH MINISTRY

- I don't have any friends my own age.
- Emotionally and socially, I relate better to adolescents.
- I'm not doing very well spiritually, and maybe this will help me get my act together.
- I'd like to keep wearing my high school letter jacket for as long as possible.
- Every other form of Christian service seems too intimidating or demanding.
- They need a youth worker, and I need a job.
- You don't expect me to go out and get a real job, do you?
- Frankly, I don't want to grow up (the Peter Pan Principle).
- I like the attention or respect or adulation (take your pick) that I get from teens.
- There is a huge need. I probably should help. No one else is stepping forward.

GOOD REASONS FOR DOING YOUTH MINISTRY

- God is opening some doors and nudging me.
- I have some gifts and experiences that could help kids.
- I'd love to accompany some teenagers on their adolescent journey in the way that older and wiser Christians accompanied me (or didn't accompany me).
- I feel a strong pull to try my hand at this.
- I really enjoy teenagers, and I love trying to help them encounter God.
- I feel eager but also scared and inadequate.
- Wise, trustworthy believers have encouraged me to give it a shot.
- I've received affirmation and confirmation that I have a knack for this.
- I see a desperate need, and I really want to help.

it blindside me? Did God "call" me? Or "guide" me? I don't know. I just know some doors closed and others opened. Desires surfaced. Abilities came to light. I emerged from my Europe-free summer with a sense that I'd discovered something important.

And so in my senior year at LSU, I gathered some friends, and we began working with youth at my campus church. At first I was a volunteer; my final semester I was a paid, part-time youth director. Upon graduation, my friends took jobs or went to law school, and I became the church's first full-time youth pastor. (More on that in the next section).

I (Dave) went to college and seminary during the days of the military draft (yes, I'm that old), and I'm pretty sure some of my classmates were motivated to go into the ministry in part by their desire to avoid the army. Through the years I've seen hints of a variety of questionable motives for doing youth ministry, ranging from being romantically attracted to one of the leaders (adult to adult, here) to simply filling a vacancy in one's home church. Certainly, every person's motives will be mixed, and we could spend an inordinate amount of time doubting ourselves and wondering. But it's essential that we have a pretty good understanding of *why* we want to work with kids.

I suppose the big question behind these details is the classic conundrum each Christian must face: What is God's will for my life?

You should ask that question in the broad, overarching sense. Maybe even read a book about the topic (there are dozens out there). But then ask the question again, this time in the narrower sense: "God, is *youth work* your will for me, at least at this juncture in my life?"

Even when we actively ask and seek and ponder, the answer can be tough to discern. Not because God doesn't want us to know. Not because he's trying to be cryptic or coy. But it's because our world is so noisy, and we're so hard of hearing.

Is youth work a good fit for you? Does it match your personality and gifts? Only God knows for sure. You'll have to feel your way. Take little steps of faith. Spend ample time listening and pondering. Be willing to experiment—and be willing to fail. You'll need to be humble enough to change course if it becomes clear you're headed down a path that's not suited for you.

Discussion Questions

1. What are your true motives—the honest reasons you have for working with youth (or wanting to do so)?

2. Through what "happening, great and small" would you say God has been sending you messages about involvement in youth ministry?

3. What's your standard operating procedure for discerning God's will for your life?

For Further Study

• Spend some time reflecting on Psalm 139:23-24. Frankly, getting still before the living God and giving him total permission to search our hearts can be a bit uncomfortable. What if he uncovers some really ugly attitudes, even some sinister motives?

• Read and ponder 1 Samuel 3:1-10. What does it mean to listen to God? How does one do this in our loud, distracting culture? What are the possibilities if we cultivate this rare habit? What happens if we don't?

Avoiding an Avoidable Mess

• Poll three or four people who know you best and love you most. Ask for some objective feedback about what they think about you working with youth.

• Before deciding to major in youth ministry at Bible college or agreeing to become a full-time youth minister, spend some time working with youth in a volunteer situation. You may discover you love it—or you may realize that what seemed like a desirable or wise option is really not for you.

When I started in ministry, I bought into the idea that student ministry was unique and didn't have to follow the mission of the church. But since then, I've embraced the idea of the student ministry existing to help fulfill the greater mission of the larger church body.

Before you sit down and start planning events, take time to create a youth ministry mission statement. Start by asking the following questions:

- Why do we do what we do?
- What has God called us to do?
- What can our student ministry do best in this community?
- What makes our student ministry unique?

And be sure to include student ministry leaders, volunteers, youth parents, and key students in this process.

The actual wording of the statement should simply describe why the ministry exists. It should be clear and concise—easy to remember. Upon completion, it should govern and guide *everything* you do.

WHAT EXACTLY IS THE *MISSION*?

In 1980, a growing (and apparently desperate) church handed me (Len) the opportunity to build a youth ministry from the ground up.

The church had been in existence for eight years. It had about 800 to 1,000 people attending Sunday worship, but it never had an official ongoing youth group, much less a designated youth director. I was the lucky—er, "blessed" guy to get the job.

So what did I do to prepare for this new ministry? Go up on a mountain—or, living in Louisiana, into a nearby swamp—for 40 days of fasting and prayer? Reread the Gospels for a refresher course in what it means to follow Christ and make disciples? Huddle with some veteran youth leaders and seek their advice? Gather all the parents of the church youth for consultation? Buy and read the five best books about working with teenagers?

I did none of that.

Instead, I went to an art supply store and bought a large piece of heavy graph paper. I borrowed several stacks of clip art and found some press-on letters. Then I sat down at a big desk with my supplies spread out in front of me and created a poster-sized calendar for our group. That was my big youth ministry "vision": An artsy yet professional-looking wall hanging that would give some semblance of spiritual structure (and meaning and hope?) to young lives. I guess I figured that if God provided Moses with two massive stone tablets to guide the children of Israel, perhaps I should have at least one oversized calendar of events to guide my students!

This was my master youth ministry plan—three months' worth of activities. And I'm talking *lots* of events: A swim party, a lock-in, a trip to the nearby zoo, Vacation Bible School for junior highers (but we gave it a catchy name: "Week in the Word"), a retreat, pizza feeds, and game nights. I tried to have something for everybody. And I had it all displayed on an eye-catching poster. What else could I possibly want or need?

Nobody ever asked me: "What's the mission behind your cool calendar? What, exactly, are you hoping to accomplish in and through all this busyness?" And I never thought to ask myself these questions either. It never occurred to me that randomness is not really a ministry strategy.

Instead, I embraced a whole host of crazy but enormously popular notions:

- Although I never thought of youth ministry as "babysitting adolescents," I was attempting to offer lots of diversions and wholesome entertainment so students would have less time to get into trouble. This was my nod to the old adage: "Idle hands are the Devil's workshop."
- I assumed that if *some* activity is good, then *more* must be better. Throw every sort of event at teenagers and surely *something* will stick to their souls.
- I hoped that for some students—at least the super-involved, the truly committed, and the attentive—participation would somehow lead to transformation; that is, their *showing up* would mystically result in their *growing up* (spiritually speaking).

In hindsight, I was a religious version of the airline pilot who announces to his passengers: "Ladies and gentlemen, this is your captain. I have some good news and some bad news. The bad news is that our navigational system is malfunctioning and we have no idea what direction we're headed. The good news, however, is that we're making record time!"

Before we start the journey, we need to be clear about where we hope to go. What is the mission we're trying to accomplish?

Share the proposed statement with your senior pastor or board to make sure the youth group mission aligns with the leadership's vision for where the church needs to go.

Once you have their support, spend time educating ministry leaders, volunteers, and students about the statement. Include the statement on your ministry's core communication pieces, such as Web sites, newsletters, and brochures.

Then use your mission statement as an ongoing tool to evaluate how proposed events and programs fit with the overall goal of the ministry. Return to your mission statement whenever you're casting vision for a new project or initiative.

—Jeff Dye

If I knew then what I know now, I'd have spent some time pondering questions like these…

Discussion Questions

1. What are the connections (and the differences) between the following oft-used terms: *Vision, mission, purpose, values, goals, objectives,* and *plans*? (You'll receive 250 youth worker bonus points for looking these up in the dictionary!)

2. If you're working in a church, what is that church's mission? If you're working with a parachurch organization, what is the stated purpose of that ministry? Is it ever legitimate or God-honoring to come into an existing organization and ignore, change, or defy its stated purpose?

3. What do you want to see happen in the lives of your students? Or, put another way, if you had to summarize God's heart for the teenagers in your group, how would you articulate what he desires to do in their lives?

For Further Study

• Take time to mull over Paul's prayers for the Ephesian believers (1:15-23 and 3:14-21). What do these prayers reveal about Paul's vision for those under his charge?

• Proverbs 19:21 says, "Many are the plans in a human heart, but it is the Lord's purpose that prevails." What are the implications of this verse for young youth workers who are wondering how and where to lead their groups?

Avoiding an Avoidable Mess

• We've all heard the popular statement, "Don't just sit there—do something!" Why might this be the wrong advice for a new youth worker?

• Take your pastor or supervisor to lunch or to the coffee shop and have a good discussion about your group. Ask this person to share his or her vision and the church or organization's mission. Take good notes. Solicit counsel. Ask the question, "If you were in my shoes right now, what course of action would you follow and why?"

WHAT IS MY *PLAN*?

Alice: Would you tell me, please, which way I ought to go from here?
Cheshire Cat: That depends a good deal on where you want to get to.
Alice: I don't much care where—
Cheshire Cat: Then it doesn't matter which way you go.
— *A conversation from Lewis Carroll's classic* Alice in Wonderland.

Everyone needs a plan, but people often plan *first* before they've considered their mission, purpose, and goals. And then the ministry looks like a grab bag of activities, lessons, and events going in no particular direction.

As stated previously, when I (Len) started out in youth ministry, I didn't exactly get "the vision" thing. I was a lot like Alice.

And since I didn't have a clear destination or goal in mind, I found planning to be difficult and frustrating. So I didn't plan very much and certainly not very far in advance.

When it came to winging it, I could wing it with the best of them. I was the king of wing. Mr. Flex. Mr. Last Minute. Playing it by ear. Going with the flow. Making it up as I went along. Hoping for the Spirit to show up.

This practice made for lots of thrills, chills, and spills, but not much satisfaction and definitely not much fruit. What I didn't grasp then (that I know now) is—

- Successful youth workers need a clear vision (a vivid mental picture of what you want your youth ministry to become).
- Successful youth leaders need specific and realistic plans that will enable them to reach their desired goals.

When I (Dave) talk with new youth pastors about their respective ministries, I often find they host events and programs simply because that's what the church has always done.

Over coffee one afternoon, I was discussing the upcoming retreat with a new junior high leader, and I asked about the "purpose" of the retreat. He asked what I meant, and I simply said, "What do you want to accomplish? What do you hope the students will learn or do because they've spent the weekend together?" He didn't have a clue.

Priscilla Steinmetz offers this wise counsel about planning as you begin a new ministry:

The first days as a new youth worker can be exciting. At long last you get to take your training, dreams, and experience and put it all into practice.

As you sit in your office (or whatever closet or hall space you've been given!) and begin planning, your head may feel as though it is going to explode. You look at the calendar—all those little boxes waiting to be filled in. It's overwhelming and time-consuming, but if we are strategic and intentional, our planning will help us reach our ultimate objectives.

We need to take into account the realities that students have assorted learning styles, differing personality types, and wildly divergent interests. The point? Refrain from a steady diet of one kind of activity. Be careful that you don't design events around things that only you enjoy or that only a few students are good at doing. When I was young, my youth pastor loved baseball, so we went to at least five games each season. This was great for those (like me) who were St. Louis Cardinal fans, but not so great for the students who didn't care for sports.

Here are a few diverse planning ideas for your consideration:

- Plan mixed gender events and separate guy-girl events.
- Plan silly and serious events.
- Plan indoor and outdoor events.
- Plan quiet, reflective events as well as loud, active, boisterous events.
- Plan spiritually light events and spiritually challenging events.
- Plan small group activities and larger group events.
- Plan some events to be held at the church and other activities to be held off site (for example, a park down the street, someone's house or camp, and so forth).

Be sure to think outside the box, too. Smaller groups of students can connect by participating in life skills events (for example, learning how to make cookies or do laundry or change the oil in the car) or athletic activities (for example, training together for a 5K run). Don't forget leadership training events. I've found that training senior high students to help with junior high students is a priceless investment.

Pray before and during your planning times to ensure that you're not planning activities just for the sake of activity. Everybody is overly busy, and nobody needs more stuff to do. Be the example to your students by planning events with eternal purpose. Make your events fill your students' souls, not just their calendars. *You won't see passion for God in your students if you have no purpose in your events.*

As a veteran youth worker, Priscilla reminds us that we must never lose sight of our mission as we plan our ministry events. It's important that we know what we're doing, but it's even more essential that we never forget *why* we're doing it.

Discussion Questions

1. Would you consider yourself a good planner? Why or why not?

2. Who is the best planner you know?

3. What are the pros and cons of planning alone versus planning with a team of coworkers?

4. What are your concrete ministry plans for the next year? For the next month? For this week? For today? How will these specific events and plans help you accomplish your ministry vision?

For Further Study

• Spend some time reading and reflecting in the Old Testament book of Nehemiah. Notice carefully Nehemiah's actions, especially in chapter two. There—before he took any action—Nehemiah carefully assessed the situation and formulated a plan for the rebuilding venture.

• Meditate on Proverbs 21:5.

• Read Acts 1:8. What was God's divine plan for the spread of the gospel?

Avoiding an Avoidable Mess

• If you know *what* you'd like to see happen with your students but you aren't exactly sure *how* to get there, then make an appointment with the individual you named in question 2 above. Ask this person to help you come up with a workable plan.

• If your area has a youth pastors' alliance, dedicate an entire meeting to swapping ideas, youth calendars, and ministry plans. Share what has worked in the past and what has flopped.

A Disney executive and an engineer were admiring the newly completed Disney World in Orlando, Florida. The monumental theme park and resort had taken more than four years to complete, and Walt Disney had passed away five years earlier. The engineer sadly shook his head and said, "If only Walt Disney could have seen this!"

The executive looked at the young engineer and said, "He did. That's why it's here."

Walt Disney's vision was so powerful that it outlasted his life. A youth minister's vision needs to be equally powerful. I wish I'd learned this earlier as a youth minister. When I started in youth ministry, my vision was about two weeks ahead.

Here are a few ideas about vision that I've picked up along the way.

• A vision brings direction to youth ministry. It's a picture of what God wants to do in and through you. A vision is not about programs but about the journey. When life gets confusing, vision is the GPS unit to keep you from getting off track.

- A vision is a blessing to parents. Your vision helps you develop a healthy partnership with parents. Parents will support your efforts when they know your heart and see clearly the God-ordained places you're headed.
- A vision helps recruit volunteers in your youth ministry. If people don't know where you're going or if they think your "big dream" is merely to organize fun events, then they're not likely to sign on. We make a mistake when we enlist volunteers by asking for drivers or cooks. Instead, we should ask for individuals who want to use their cars and culinary skills to make an eternal difference in the lives of students.
- A vision creates passion in students. It can get apathetic teenagers involved in serving in their youth group, not just being spectators.

—*Todd Smith*

- Attend a Youth Specialties national convention or training workshop. You'll receive more creative and field-tested ideas than you can use in a lifetime.

WHAT ARE MY *EXPECTATIONS?*

Consider the following scenario.

As the new youth worker in town, you arrive at the church to high expectations. Everyone is confident they'll soon have "hundreds saved and thousands healed." People are pretty sure a youth revival is coming—and you're the new Billy Graham. Well, not exactly, but you feel the pressure—to perform, to draw kids, and to perform.

Of course, you arrive with all kinds of ideas in your bag of tricks (games, media, illustrations, talks)—some you learned in school, others that always worked for you in past ministry settings, and even some new ones you read about online. You're anxious to give them all a try—and you do.

Some of your ideas work. Some don't. But eventually the bag is empty. You can repeat a trick only so many times. The honeymoon ends. After about a year and a half, you pack it in and move to the next gig (highly expectant church).

Nothing is wrong with "flash"—excitement, fun, and entertainment. But it can take you only so far. In order to have lasting effects—changed lives—it will take much more.

Jesus provides the model for us. Consider his entrance into the world—pretty humble. Thirty years later, his public ministry began quietly, slowly. There was very little flash at first. Even his first few miracles were somewhat private. Eventually, crowds gathered and ministry groupies clamored to get close to him, but he didn't start out that way.

So what was Jesus' approach to ministry, his strategy? He built relationships. And that takes time.

Beware of anyone who tells you how much you can accomplish in your first year of youth ministry. First impressions and building a ministry foundation are vital. But the solid accomplishments of that first year usually don't come from the flashy stuff.

Relationships—with students, parents, volunteers, church leaders, and others—take time to begin, develop, and deepen. And you'll need to spend time communicating your ministry philosophy and values and casting vision. So give yourself a break from unrealistic expectations.

Did you know that every disappointment in life stems from unmet expectations? Every single one.

It's a fact of life: The difference between what you *expect* and what you *experience* is the degree to which you feel disappointed.

So if you want to avoid constant disappointment in youth ministry, it's important to keep your expectations in line with reality. Here are some principles to remember.

- Youth are fickle. This is because people are fickle and teenagers are (contrary to the beliefs of some) young *people*. Therefore, we're asking for trouble when we expect more from our students than they're able to give.
- Bigger isn't always better. More isn't always better either. Find other ways to keep score besides raw numbers.
- All good things take time. (Think of oak trees and smoked ribs and diamonds.)
- Since we can't see into hearts or know what tomorrow holds, many of our conclusions about events and people are premature—and wrong.
- You can't control people or outcomes. So one of the ways to guarantee disappointment and frustration is to try to play God.
- You can only do what you can do.
- There is a big difference between *hoping* for something ("It would be so cool if we

After working in four churches, this is what I've discovered: The youth ministry didn't start humming, didn't get to the point where I was remotely content with what was going on, until my third year. It took that long to infiltrate the system with the vision and strategy God had given me. It took at least that long to build an effective volunteer team. It took that long to build trust with parents and boards and the senior pastor. It took that long to know the culture of the community and the local church.

So relax. Give yourself some time. You still have to run a program. But focus on the foundational stuff: Establishing relationships, locating and building student and adult leadership, casting vision, and communicating values.

—*Mark Oestreicher*

TEN REASONABLE EXPECTATIONS OF YOUTH MINISTRY

1. Your patience will be tried.
2. Your heart will be broken.
3. Your head will throb.
4. Your stomach will hurt (from laughter, from stress, and from eating too much junk food and fast food).
5. Your strength will be depleted, and your muscles will ache.
6. Your wisdom will be inadequate.
7. Your maturity and actions and decisions will be questioned.
8. Your feelings will be hurt.
9. Your pay will be low.
10. Your students will love and appreciate you (but most will never tell you so).

had 20 kids sign up for this mission trip.") and *demanding* something ("If I don't get 20 kids to agree to go on this mission trip, then that proves (a) I'm a lousy leader and I should quit; (b) These kids don't love God, and I should ream out the whole group at our next meeting; or (c) Both a and b!").

So keep it real. That's a good principle for your expectations *and* your ministry.

Discussion Questions

1. How do we balance our desire for effectiveness and the promises of the Bible (the ones that encourage us to "ask for big things and trust God to bless us") with the realities of working with sinful people who aren't always so cooperative?

2. What are you hoping will happen in your ministry to students over the next, say, 12 months?

3. What unrealistic expectations might you have when thinking about your youth ministry?

For Further Study

• Spend some time reflecting on Ephesians 3:20-21. What does it say about God? What are some applications of these verses for a young

youth worker who's eager to see God do great and mighty things in the lives of students?

• Read 2 Corinthians, Paul's most personal letter. In it, he talks candidly about the ministry—what it entails and what kinds of difficulties a minister can expect. Warning: It's not for the faint of heart!

Avoiding an Avoidable Mess

• Invite the most experienced youth worker in town to lunch. Pick this person's brain. Talk about the whole subject of expectations. Ask, "What should I expect as I begin youth ministry?"

• Each morning, hold up your daily schedule or to-do list as an offering to God, saying, "Not my will, but yours be done."

I (Len) am at the Rangers Ballpark in Arlington, Texas, with 11 junior high guys and two adult male volunteers. We're midway through a weeklong summer mission trip. Today, we conducted Backyard Bible Clubs at a couple of lower-income apartment complexes. Tonight, we've come to watch the Texas Rangers play the Oakland A's.

The girls in our group are still back at the church building that we're calling home this week. They're showering, drying their hair, and applying makeup. When we left them, they looked like 13-year-old girls. When they arrive—about midway through the second inning would be my best guess—they'll probably look like 18-year-old women.

While the girls wanted to clean up before heading to the game, the guys had different priorities. They insisted we be here at 5 p.m.—the moment the gates open—because they know batting practice offers the best chance to get autographs.

So while my fellow chaperones check out the assorted food options, I sit by myself in a shady section of the mostly empty stadium. Though it's 5:30 in the evening, the temperature is still in the mid-90s. I can see most of our boys clustered around the Rangers' dugout with markers in hand and hopeful, almost angelic looks on their faces. Every few seconds the distinctive crack of bat meeting ball fills the air. Every few minutes I see the boys cluster suddenly, high-five one another, and gawk at a new signature on one of their hats or gloves.

What fascinates me most, however, is the extensive warmup regimen the players put themselves through down on the field. I might begin a workout by making a few big circles with my arms and maybe twisting my torso back and forth for a few seconds. But not these guys. They take "limbering up" to a whole new level. Every ligament, joint, and muscle gets serious attention. In fact, the thorough stretching process takes some of them more than 45 minutes to complete.

Upon further reflection, it makes perfect sense. *Of course* these players go to such lengths. They're in a business where physical health is everything. If they enter the game carelessly—without being physically ed—they might tweak a hamstring or pull an oblique (whatever is). Then they'd be sitting in the dugout or on the disabled list for weeks, maybe even months. When their million-dollar bodies aren't healthy and in tiptop shape, they can't help the team.

What a valuable reminder this is for folks in youth ministry. How can we honestly expect to deal with students' hearts if we aren't tending to our own? When we ignore our internal spiritual condition and focus only on external physical demands, we become susceptible to a host of spiritual dangers.

If I knew then what I know now, I'd want someone to tell me—or at least remind me—to beware of the following soul care mistakes...

SOUL CARE MISTAKE 1: EMPHASIZING DOING MORE THAN BEING

If having a lot to do means a person is important, then most new youth directors feel pretty special. Here was a typical day's to-do list from my (Len) first job in youth ministry:

- ❏ Breakfast with student leaders
- ❏ Meet with concerned mom about her wayward daughter
- ❏ Reserve vans for weekend retreat
- ❏ Check on new group T-shirts
- ❏ Review new youth curriculum samples
- ❏ Prep for Wednesday night talk
- ❏ Church staff meeting during lunch
- ❏ Discipleship time with college volunteers
- ❏ Work out with ninth-grade guys
- ❏ Dinner
- ❏ Attend JV basketball game at the high school

Different days featured different stuff—but every day was similarly full. So many students. So many needs. So many meetings and activities and events. That's the nature of the beast, right? That's the thing about being a youth minister—you actually have to minister to youth! You're like the ringmaster of some crazy, three-ring circus.

There's only one problem: How do you care for others when your own heart is dry?

Everybody wants something. Everybody needs something. Some teenagers long for what they don't really need; others don't want what they really need. So you engage. You look at their faces, and you study their lives. Once in a while, you get a fleeting glimpse of their messy, desperate hearts. Grand Canyons of need. So huge. So diverse.

You dive in and start giving. Counsel. Affirmation. A smile. Correction. A hug. A few minutes of undivided attention. A wise word. A warm pat on the back. A loving-but-firm kick in the butt. An invitation into community. A scholarship to the retreat. And, hopefully, a clearer picture of who God is.

You start each day motivated—and challenged. By day's end you feel weary and overwhelmed and, if you're like me, maybe a tad guilty. Too many unchecked boxes. *Couldn't I have made one more phone call? Helped one more person?* So the next day's list is a bit longer. You resolve to multitask more efficiently. Maybe you can skip the workout—or at least quit working out with a bunch of ninth-grade goof-offs who waste so much time!

The days become weeks and blur into months. And then you notice it. You're spent. You have nothing left. You speak to the group not because you have something to say, but because you have to say something. You've got no meaningful counsel to give. No energy to build relationships. Zero motivation or passion. Little things start to bug you. You get testy, prickly, irritable. You daydream about escaping. Little temptations begin to trip you up.

Meanwhile, the needs never stop. Students find new and more creative ways to get into trouble. The ministry machine you helped create lurches forward, dragging you with it. God feels distant and impersonal—more like a nice idea than a close friend. Your foundational beliefs seem like abstract theories. You start to resent everyone and everything. You moan about your ragged life and maybe even start checking the want ads.

Proverbs 4:23 urges: "Above all else, guard your heart, for it is the wellspring of life" (NIV). This is Solomon speaking, the ancient king of Israel who is universally regarded as the wisest man ever. He's sharing with his sons what he's learned in life.

The "heart" of which Solomon speaks is a hugely important concept in the Bible. In fact, the terms *heart* and *hearts* occur some 950 times! A few of these instances are literal references to the blood-pumping organ in the center of our chests. Most, however, refer metaphorically to the central essence of a person—that immaterial seat of the *emotions* (see Proverbs 12:25; 13:12; 14:13), *intellect* (15:14, 28); and *will* (5:12). It's worth noting that the ancient Hebrews did not draw sharp distinctions between the terms *heart, soul,* and *mind.* For them these words blurred and overlapped; in some places, they seem to be used interchangeably.

In the biblical understanding, the heart is the place where we reflect and dream and desire and wrestle with beliefs and ideas—ultimately forming our attitudes, values, and convictions. Our hearts are where we feel, processing or burying painful events, as well as experiencing pleasant emotions. Finally, it's there in our hearts, at the deepest level of our beings, that we choose how we'll live, where we'll go, and what we'll do.

You could think of your heart as your thinker, feeler, and chooser. To use a computer analogy, the heart is like the motherboard, operating system, and hard drive of your life—all rolled into one.

This is why Solomon says the heart is the "wellspring" of life. The Hebrew word means *starting point*. In other words, the heart is the source from which everything else flows. Taint the spring at its starting point, and the water downstream will be undrinkable and unhealthy. Are you starting to get the picture? Your heart is *everything*.

This is why, of course, Solomon says, "above all else, guard" your heart. Your heart is infinitely more important than the next big youth event. Your heart must take precedence over any and every meeting. Your heart matters more than all those urgent "to dos" in your Black-berry. How can you help a teenager stay afloat when you're going under for the third time?

"Above *all else*"—could Solomon speak any more clearly about the priority of caring for your own soul? We have to guard our hearts—not in the sense of being walled off or aloof from people but rather watching over our own souls. Monitoring our spiritual health. Looking for signs of slippage, evidence of danger. Being ever vigilant, wary, and alert. Our hearts matter above all else because everything—our attitudes, values, words, and actions—stems from the heart.

Ministry is, first and foremost, a matter of the heart. What's your youth group's biggest need? A frantic leader who's so busy *doing* that she has no time for *being*? Or a purposeful, in-the-moment leader filled with all the fullness of God (Ephesians 3:19)?

Discussion Questions

1. To what part of the first-person account above do you most relate?

2. How can you tell when you've neglected your heart?

3. Most Christians are aware of the truths described above—caring for one's heart isn't a new concept. So why do we keep falling into the same stupid trap?

4. What are some practical ways that fellow ministry colleagues can help one another avoid this condition?

For Further Study
• Read 1 Kings 19:1-18. The prophet Elijah has just done vigorous spiritual battle with a host of false prophets on Mount Carmel. King Ahab and Queen Jezebel are threatening his life. Elijah is fearful and exhausted. Notice how God ministers to him.

• Read and ponder Mark 6:30-44. This is the account of Jesus trying to take his disciples on a much-needed retreat after a busy time of ministry. Take some time to imagine Jesus speaking the words from verse 31 to you. How does it affect you to know that Jesus cares deeply for the well being of your soul?

Avoiding an Avoidable Mess
• Commit Proverbs 4:23 to memory: "Above all else, guard your heart, for it is the wellspring of life."

• Take your schedule to a trusted confidante, mentor, or ministry colleague and get some honest feedback. Have a straightforward discussion about priorities. Brainstorm together 10 ways that you could better care for your souls.

• Begin the daily practice of *lectio divina* (Latin for "divine reading"). This is an ancient spiritual discipline that involves reading and meditating on a short Bible passage several times with a goal of really hearing what God is saying to you through that particular Scripture. A great book that teaches this practice is *Enjoy the Silence: A 30-Day Experiment in Listening to God* by Duffy and Maggie Robbins (Zondervan/Youth Specialties, 2005). This book was actually written for youth, but it's a great resource for youth leaders, too.

SOUL CARE MISTAKE 2: LETTING YOUR WELL RUN DRY
Back in the mid-'80s, I (Len) drove a blue Honda Civic 5-speed. It was a great little car. (With current gasoline prices, I wish I still had it!) But after a few years, it began to misfire and run rough. When I took it in for service, the mechanic told me there was sediment in the gas tank. Whenever I drove around with the needle on "empty" (as I usually did), some of that gunk would get into the engine. The mechanic told me I

could eliminate the problem by keeping my gas tank at least halfway full. And sure enough when I did that, the sputtering went away.

The analogy isn't perfect. But in a similar way, when our spiritual tank is near the empty mark, what's left in our souls is mostly sludge. Even little demands result in big unpleasant reactions.

I discovered this truth very early in my first summer ministry internship. We were taking kids on a late-May beach excursion. School had just let out. There were about 30 kids, ranging from seventh through twelfth grade, and a handful of adults. As I looked out the school bus window, I tried to soak it all in: The cloudless blue sky, the endless white sand, and the inviting blue-green waters of the Gulf of Mexico. I could feel the morning breeze on my skin. I could smell that intoxicating mix of salty sea air and coconut tanning oil. As the driver maneuvered to park, I closed my eyes, leaned back in my seat, and smiled. *Life is good,* I thought. *I'm getting paid to hang out with kids. Amazing.*

My job description that summer was varied. Lead weekly Wednesday night gatherings for the junior high kids. Help plan and pull off a wide assortment of other youth events. Hang out, be available, teach, run errands (in New Orleans, a really cool city), dream up and act in crazy skits, and other fun stuff. My mind was whirring. I was excited to try out all my brilliant ideas, put to use all my experiences, utilize my—ahem—theological wisdom. And it would all begin in the sun and sand of the gorgeous Gulf.

After Bill, the church youth pastor, gave a few obligatory rules and safety warnings and went over the day's schedule, our driver leaned over and yanked the bus door open. Excited kids burst out onto the sand. Boys raced to see who'd be first to get in the water. Self-conscious girls clustered awkwardly by the bus door, waiting for friends who could give one last bathing-suit check.

As I stepped into the sunshine, shaking my head at the wonder of it all, I heard someone call my name. I turned just in time to get two heaping handfuls of dry sand right in the face. Welcome to youth ministry, Len.

I yelped and went down on all fours. With my eyes burning, now filled with grit, I couldn't see a thing. But I could hear Brad, one of our seventh graders, hooting hysterically; and I could tell he was only a few feet away from me. Like a wounded, enraged animal, I lunged instinctively toward the laughter. I grabbed a leg and yanked Brad down into the sand beside me.

I didn't punch or choke him. (I was tempted.) I didn't smash sand in his face (although the thought did cross my mind). I didn't let fly a single expletive. (Do I get any points for showing a smidge of self-control?)

HOW TO BURN OUT IN YOUTH MINISTRY

1. Work 80-plus hours every week and never take a vacation or a day off.
2. Make sure you stay so busy that you don't have time for God. A good formula to follow is to spend 98 percent of your time and energy running around telling kids how wonderful it is to have a personal relationship with God, leaving 2 percent of your time and energy for your own relationship with him.
3. If you're married, remember: Your ministry comes before your spouse. If you're single: Don't develop a social life of your own. Spend all your time with teenagers.
4. Spend lots of time thinking about the things you can't buy with the money you're not making.
5. Whatever else you do, make sure you entertain your students. How else will kids learn?
6. Don't read anything that doesn't pertain directly to your ministry.

None of that mattered as I sat on Brad's chest, yelling at him. I was giving everyone— all the wide-eyed girls, plus Bill and most of the adult volunteers a sneak peek into my untended soul. In the crazy weeks leading up to this moment—days spent taking final exams, moving out of my college apartment, making a quick visit home, and relocating to the metro New Orleans area—I'd neglected to care for my soul. And in a sudden, stressful moment, the truth about my disordered soul came out.

Ever wish you could have a do-over? I do. I wish all the time that I could go back to certain, specific, less-than-stellar ministry moments with the insight I have now (or am starting to have).

Thankfully, that episode on the beach didn't ruin my ministry. After a few seconds of verbal fireworks, I came to my senses, and a giant wave of shame washed over me. Everything got really quiet and awkward. Embarrassed onlookers quickly and quietly slipped away. With Bill mediating, Brad and I talked briefly, seeking out and granting forgiveness to each other. I spent the next hour trying to wash the sand out my eyes—and spent the rest of the day asking God to wash the gunk out of my heart.

Bottom line? Whatever is in our hearts will come to the surface of our lives eventually. If we're daily spending time with Christ, if we're stopping to remember what's true, if we're nourishing our souls with God's Word, if we're opening our hearts to the Spirit, and if we're surrendering our agendas and our wills to what God is doing, then, and only then, we'll experience what Jesus promised in John 7:37-39—personal refreshment that overflows into the lives of others, blessing them.

Discussion Questions

1. When's the last time you said or did something you wish you could take back? What happened?

2. Certainly trials and tough times develop character, but difficulties also reveal character. How have you responded this week to minor irritations? Moderate problems? Major crises?

3. Everybody blows it eventually. And while we can always apologize profusely for wrong words and actions, we cannot undo them. If the intern in the story above were your friend (or one of your youth staffers), what counsel would you give? How would you handle this situation?

For Further Study
• Spend some time reflecting on Matthew 23:25-28.

• Read and ponder 1 Timothy 4:7. Note the verb Paul uses when he challenges his young protégé: "Train yourself to be godly." What intentional practices are you cultivating?

• If you haven't already, take a few minutes to memorize 1 John 1:9—"If we confess our sins, he is faithful and just and will forgive us our sins and purify us from all unrighteousness." You're going to need it—a lot!

Avoiding an Avoidable Mess
• Remember the reality of entropy. In a fallen world, things continually tend toward disorder.

• As a youth worker, you can "train yourself to be godly." Through consistent spiritual practices (prayer, Bible reading, meditation, and so forth), it's possible to gradually develop a heart and a life marked by the fruit of the Spirit (love, joy, peace, patience, kindness, goodness, faithfulness, gentleness, and self control). John Ortberg's book *The Life You've Always Wanted* (Zondervan, 1997, 2002) is a great introduction to a life of spiritual discipline.

7. Never associate with other youth ministers, especially outside your denomination.
8. If possible, eat every meal at McDonald's. I recommend Quarter Pounders with cheese, large fries, and chocolate shakes.
9. Don't delegate—after all, no one can do your work quite the way you can.
10. Never ask anything of your kids. Teach them that it's okay just to soak up everything you say, like good little sponges.
11. Expect immediate results. If you don't get them, you're obviously not called to youth ministry.
12. Above all else, remember: The most important thing is *numbers*. When Jesus said, "Feed my sheep," what he really meant was, "Count 'em."

If you are careful to obey these commandments and write them on your heart, I can guarantee you a quick and complete burnout.
—*Kent Keller*

• Form an accountability partnership with another trusted soul or two. It might be a fellow youth worker or an older mentor-type figure. Pick out three or four agreed-upon questions to ask one another every week or two.

SOUL CARE MISTAKE 3: NOT LEARNING TO SAY "NO!"

In my (Dave) Campus Life days, we had an annual fall event, "Scream in the Dark," that involved creating a haunted house by doing some serious renovations to an abandoned house to make it scary and safe (up to code). My staff and I worked serious hours every day tearing holes in walls, painting, and constructing—in addition to our normal ministry activities. And then, once the haunted house opened, our daily schedule included arriving at the house around noon to clean up and repair from the previous night, and then we'd work straight through 'til 11 p.m. We'd manage for a while, especially with great volunteer help. But I remember falling into bed bone-tired, getting up the next day, going to the office and campus (when I could), and then heading back to the house for another long day.

After just a few days of this, I was sick, cranky, and thinking about leaving the ministry. And I wasn't alone. That's when a wise and observant board member took me aside and set me straight. He pointed out that although our motives were good and our efforts commendable, our values and priorities were upside down. We were busy but neglecting ourselves, our families, and our real reason for being in ministry—the kids. We needed to scale back and design a healthier schedule.

You can't do *everything*. Nearly every veteran youth worker has stories to share about the importance of learning how to say "no"—and the dangers of failing to do so.

Read these wise words from Priscilla Steinmetz:

> You don't have to do youth ministry for very long to know that it can be physically, mentally, and emotionally exhausting. It can also wipe you out spiritually—especially if you make the mistake of trying to do everything.
>
> During my years of ministry, both as a single and a married person, at times I've looked into the mirror and had a hard time finding me (like when you get out of the shower and steam covers the mirror). In those times it's as if my whole being is lost. All my thoughts, time, and energy are consumed with ministry issues.
>
> I've learned that in the midst of pouring myself into students and volunteers, I have to acquire the spiritual discipline of saying "no." This practice of setting personal limits is hard, but it's spiritually necessary and ultimately beneficial to all.

After one long period of feeling overwhelmed and not taking time for myself, I discovered that the reason I didn't want to say "no" was because of pride in my own heart. My pride stemmed from thinking that I'm here to personally minister to *every* student. I forgot that youth ministry is not about me; it's about the saving grace of God. The simple fact is that *God* is in control. He desires to work in me and through me to love students. But he cannot do that if I neglect my own heart. The familiar words of Psalms 139 have helped me identify (and say "no" to) pride in my life.

Dealing with prideful thinking is a primary way I guard my heart. It keeps me from feeling overwhelmed by the foolish pressure to "save the world."

It's normal to be scared to say "no." We don't want our students, their parents, our bosses, or our volunteers to think we don't care. But at the same time we also don't want to teach them to neglect *their* hearts either. If we want those who are touched by our ministries to live fully and richly, then we must show them how. We must embrace a lifestyle marked by a healthy work-rest rhythm.

John O'Leary adds his own story about the importance of realizing your limits:

This weekend I got a phone call that some kids in my group were in an abusive situation, and I engaged. I was on the phone for a couple of hours. But at some point, I've got to walk away and say, "I can't *save* them; I can't *fix* that situation; I can only *help* it." At some point I have to go and spend time with my own family.

Sometimes you get deep into it and spend time with people and try to work the situation. But eventually you just have to walk away and say, "That's what I can do. Now, Lord, please use that." But you have to walk away.

A few years ago my wife bought me (Len) a hammock during a stressful period of ministry. I think I used it maybe 10 times in three years. Eventually, I noticed some sparrows were pulling cotton threads out of the hammock's cords. Later on it struck me that maybe the God who takes care of the birds told them: "Hey, since 'Mr. Important' is too busy 'saving the world' to appreciate this blessing I gave him, why don't you guys at least get some use out of it? Go ahead. Help yourself. Build your nests with it. Enjoy!"

Discussion Questions

1. Psychologists speak of certain people having a "messiah complex." What do they mean by this phrase?

2. On a scale of 1 to 10, with 1 meaning "I have *no* problems saying 'no' (in fact, I need to be saying 'yes!' more often than I do)" and 10 meaning "I am a certified workaholic with an overexaggerated sense of my own self-importance," how would you rate yourself?

3. How might saying "No!" actually be a powerful act of simple faith?

4. What practical guidelines have you developed for knowing when to say, "That's all I can do—and all I should do"?

For Further Study

• Spend some time reflecting on the concept of Sabbath rest (Genesis 2:1-3). How can the cessation of work be a holy thing?

• Mark 1:34 makes a point of saying that Jesus healed "*many* who had various diseases" (emphasis added)—in other words, Jesus did *not* heal "all." In Mark 6:31, surrounded by countless people with a variety of deep needs, Jesus told his followers, "Come with me by yourselves to a quiet place and get some rest." What implications does this statement have for our lives?

Avoiding an Avoidable Mess

Priscilla Steinmetz offers these simple strategies she's learned over the years to help youth workers who are taking on more than God intends.

PERSONAL STRATEGIES

• **Remember that God sees and knows.** God knows your heart—that you ache at the thought of not having enough time or energy for all the students in your ministry.
• **Don't confuse work for God and time with God.** It's easy to get so busy writing lessons and praying for your students' needs that you neglect your own heart.
• **Plan with purpose.** Structure your own personal time the same way you plan ministry events—with purpose. Schedule a weekly date night with your spouse (or with friends if you aren't married). Guard this time fiercely.

- **Don't clutter the calendar.** When your students are celebrating holidays with their families, you should, too!
- **Call on idea people to engage.** When you feel overwhelmed, instead of getting defensive ("I can't do even one more thing!"), get smart ("That's a great idea! Would you be willing to organize and host such an event for our group?") Encourage and teach students and parents to host events on their own. Not only does this challenge others to step up, use their gifts, and get involved, but it also removes the unnecessary pressure that you personally must do everyone's bidding.
- **Utilize available resources.** You'll be able to take long deep breaths if you wisely take advantage of all the resources around you.
- **Develop a team.** Face it: You're not equipped to meet every potential student need. By having a volunteer network of both genders and with assorted abilities and backgrounds, you'll have a better youth ministry, and you'll end up less stressed.
- **Utilize older, sharper students.** Investing time and energy into training student leaders will strengthen and build support for your program.
- **Be innovative.** Try new things. Think outside the box. Work smarter, not just harder.
- **Think ahead.** If you have students who just want to hang out with you, bring them along on errands or have them help you with projects.

SOUL CARE MISTAKE 4: TRYING TO WIN IN THE TRENCHES WITHOUT GREAT SUPPORT BEHIND THE FRONT LINES

Often, youth work is just plain fun—spending time with teenagers who are so full of life, doing stupid goofy things with balloons and shaving cream, playing practical jokes, teasing and being teased. Yet the lighthearted laughter that dominates so many days can obscure a deeper reality: Youth work is *war*.

I know, I know—that sounds over-the-top melodramatic. But it's a great truth. It is, to borrow a phrase from the late great Christian philosopher Francis Schaeffer, a true truth.

Youth ministry is war. It is a life-or-death struggle for young souls. It is a fierce conflict with malevolent forces that function like spiritual terrorists.

When I (Len) began working with teenagers, I would have said I believed that. But I'm not sure I was *deeply* convinced; at least not enough to be jarred into action on a daily basis. Let's be honest: In a room full of laughing teenagers, we can easily forget the grim truth that a battle rages all around us. But that doesn't make it any less true.

Take that circle of students doing the Hokey Pokey and acting all dorky at your group's "Nerd Night." The muscular kid is Andrew. He's a talented jock and a great kid—a great kid who happens to be scarred for life because his grandpa molested him repeatedly. He hides it pretty well, don't you think? Next to him is April, a cute, shy tenth grader who fights a daily battle with depression. We could go all the way around the circle, but you get the idea. As my friend Walt Wiley likes to say, there's a drama behind every face. Behind the smiles are addictions, mood disorders, and family dysfunction.

Spiritual conflict differs from literal, physical war in one big way: Its effects aren't readily evident. A teenager may appear to have it all together. He may act like he doesn't have a care in the world. She may come from the "perfect" home, attend every event, and give rock-solid answers during Bible discussions. Still, each kid, every single one, qualifies for a Purple Heart. They are the walking wounded. And every day the Enemy continues—and intensifies—his attacks. Another kid walks into an ambush. Your sharpest student takes a bullet and goes down.

This means that the job of a youth worker—your job—is to be vigilant, courageous, and heroic. You are, and this is not meant to be a joke, a spiritual version of Jack Bauer.

Now, just in case you've been living on an Amish farm for the last decade, Jack Bauer is a special agent with the Counter Terrorist Unit (CTU) on the hit Fox TV series *24*. Jack is every terrorist's worst nightmare. And because he represents such a threat to their evil intentions, he's a constant target. The bad guys are always trying to take him out. This means Jack has a daunting, two-part job description: Stay alive and well...so he can continue fighting for others.

Now, as capable and resourceful as Jack Bauer is, he'd never try to engage the enemy all by himself. Viewers know he relies heavily on an amazing team of competent and committed fellow agents—the crew back at the CTU headquarters. Apparently, Jack's cell phone enjoys exceptional network coverage because he can—and does—phone CTU from anywhere and everywhere. While firing off rounds with the gun in his left hand, Jack is constantly making calls with his right—phoning in air strikes and getting satellite imagery or real-time camera feeds or even building blueprints. Whenever Jack has a need, he speed-dials Chloe, the snarly computer whiz back at headquarters. She provides help in a snap. Between car chases and defusing dirty bombs, Jack even calls and chats with the President four or five times a day.

If I could go back to when I was starting out in youth ministry, one thing I'd want to do differently is to really wrestle with this reality of spiritual conflict. I hope I'd allow God to pierce my heart daily with the sobering truth that youth ministry is not all fun and games. It's also a serious struggle for souls. If I could get a do-over, I'd purposely create a CTU-like team of prayer warriors.

The great preacher and author John Piper insists that this is precisely the purpose of prayer. Prayer is essentially calling in a powerful air strike from heaven as we battle here on earth with the forces of evil. Prayer is like a spiritual cell phone that always works and connects us with all the resources of headquarters—even to God himself.

Please don't make the mistake of believing you can win the war in the trenches without receiving great help *behind the front lines*. For the sake of your own soul, and for the sake of your students, establish your ministry on a solid base of intercessory prayer.

Discussion Questions

1. What five adjectives best describe your personal prayer habits?

2. Alfred Lord Tennyson once claimed, "More things are wrought by prayer than this world dreams of." If that's true (and the Bible assures us it is), then why don't youth leaders pray more urgently and more consistently for their ministries?

3. Who are the pray-ers in your church—the really committed intercessors?

For Further Study

• Read and reflect on Ephesians 6:10-18. What in this well-known passage jumps out at you about spiritual conflict?

• Spend some time contemplating Exodus 17:8-13. While Joshua fights a battle down in the valley, Moses remains up on the mountain with his arms propped up, raising his staff as a symbol of calling for and trusting in divine intervention. Jot down the spiritual lessons you find here.

Avoiding an Avoidable Mess

• Among your first acts, recruit a prayer team. Find some hard-core prayer warriors—praying moms and dads, grandmas and grandpas— who will daily lift up you and your students before God. Keep them current on what's happening (or needs to be happening). Email them new, specific prayer requests each week.

• Take 20 minutes a day to pray for the students in your group and the volunteers on your team. Even better, find a different prayer partner for each day of the workweek (Monday through Friday) who will agree to meet you for 30 minutes of prayer time. This will ensure that your ministry is covered in prayer.

SOUL CARE MISTAKE 5: NOT BEING READY FOR THE EMOTIONAL TRAPS OF YOUTH MINISTRY

Check out these confessions from actual youth workers. Stories like this are very common:

- "I was on full-time staff at my first church. I'd been there about a year. Granted, it was a large church and unbelievably disorganized. And add the fact that I never got any Sunday morning platform time. Ever. But still, imagine how I felt when our leaders conducted a congregational survey and three church members said we could greatly improve our church if we'd just hire a full-time youth director. Talk about feeling invisible and irrelevant!"
- "Many of my college peers went into secular careers and made twice, triple, and—in a few cases—even quadruple my income. Over the years, I've watched some of my *students* finish college, go through law school or med school, and now at age 30 they're living a lifestyle I'll never have. On a youth minister's salary, I know I can't afford to give my family certain things and experiences. That really bugs me. It probably shouldn't. But it does. A lot."
- "Nobody prepared me for how harsh kids can be. I remember back in college I was working with this one group, and we piled into somebody's car to go somewhere. There were probably six of us crammed into the backseat. Suddenly, there is this lull in the conversation, and this one girl—Kim was her name—stares at my face from like a foot away and announces in a loud voice, "Oh, sick! You've got a humongous zit on your nose!" I was so embarrassed. I was thinking, *Gee, thanks for pointing that out. Like I hadn't noticed it every time I looked in the mirror for the last three days!* I would say that if you plan to work with teenagers, you'd better have thick skin because kids will blurt out whatever comes into their heads."
- "When the girls I'd worked with since they were seventh graders graduated from high school this past May, I felt this overwhelming sadness. I was so close to those eight or ten girls. But my little group suddenly all scattered. We keep in touch—Facebook and all that. But it's not the

same. And as much as I love student ministry, I find myself thinking, *I just don't know if I can keep doing this. Giving my heart to a whole new batch of girls, only to have them walk right out of my life.* The thought of starting over with a new group just depresses me."

- "You want to know what bugs me? When you're really in a kid's life, and you know him—all his hopes and dreams, all his issues and struggles. And then the kid starts acting out, and who do the parents make an appointment to see? Not you. Your boss. They go over your head or around you, like you're suddenly invisible. Like you have nothing worthwhile to say."

- "In a parent meeting, this one mom just went off on me. I don't even remember what she said, what her beefs were. Maybe they were legit. But it was her tone. So condescending. So disrespectful. Just total contempt—like I was a complete idiot. Fortunately, she was so out of bounds that I think all the other parents felt protective of me. Anyway, despite feeling totally humiliated (and pretty ticked), God must have given me an infusion of grace because I somehow answered her respectfully and softly (which is *not* what I was feeling inside)."

- "One year, on my staff director's birthday, I watched people go nuts giving him stuff. And it wasn't even like it was his 40th or 50th birthday—some milestone. He was turning 44 or some random age like that. A few months later, when my birthday came, nobody said a word. Nobody did a thing. Not that I expected some huge fuss, but a simple card would have been nice. I mean, I know he's a great guy and all, but what am I—chopped liver?"

- "I remember when I told my dad I was going to work with youth. He got this pained expression on his face. He shook his head and shut his eyes like he was having a migraine or something. Heavy sighs, the whole deal. He made several derogatory comments, but the main one I remember is, 'All right, go ahead and get this little Mother Teresa fantasy out of your system, but then I want you to get a real job, okay?'"

- "For several years, I poured into this one kid. I mean we were super close. You maybe could accuse me of not paying adequate attention to other kids—but not this one. I was at his house, his games—all the time. Really in his life. When he went off to college, we stayed in close touch. And now when it's time for him to get married, who gets asked to do his premarital counseling, to perform his wedding? The senior pastor—who barely even knows him. I guess that shouldn't bug me. But it does. It hurts. It feels like a rejection. Like, 'Now that it's time for this big event, we're turning to the real pro.'"

The youth workers above have collided with a great and mysterious reality: *Working with students means navigating an emotional minefield.* Every day, crazy stuff happens. Some of it is good leaving you with a sense of joy, fulfillment, satisfaction, or hope. On most days, however, events will unfold, and you'll sense powerful emotions like anger, hurt, sadness, or confusion surging through your soul. You might be rejected, taken for granted, unappreciated, or disrespected. All that just comes with the territory.

So, lest you fall prey to the emotional roller-coaster ride that is youth ministry, here are some practical suggestions and reminders:

Understand that working with young people involves the whole gamut of strong emotions. If you don't want a job that requires emotional involvement, you may want to forget youth ministry and get a job pushing paper or pecking away on a computer. Someone said once (about parenthood): "The decision to have a child is momentous. It is like going through life with your heart outside your body." We could amend that to say that the decision to work with teens is momentous— like walking around with your heart exposed. If you minister to students, then you'll experience a whole range of powerful emotions.

Understand that youth workers don't always have the greatest reputation. Granted, stereotypes aren't fair, and they're surely not 100 percent accurate. But they do exist and often have some basis. Deservedly or not, you'll get lumped in with every impulsive, irresponsible, and slightly goofy youth pastor who's preceded you. Kids, parents, school administrators, and others will all have some image of what a youth minister is. And they'll automatically assume you fit that image. That means it's up to you to rewrite the image.

Understand that all ministry involves a pecking order. People pay attention (probably too much attention) to titles and organizational charts. This means the guy or gal at the top will get more respect, more clout, more pay, and more perks than the folks who fall lower on the totem pole. To borrow an analogy from chess, senior pastors and ministry heads are the kings; youth pastors and volunteer workers are pawns. Stick with it a while and you may eventually move beyond pawn-dom; you might one day be viewed as a knight, or possibly even a bishop or a rook. But you'll never be regarded by the masses in the same way that your superiors are viewed.

Understand that youth ministry is not a career path that pays big bucks.[1] It ranks right in there with teaching and beginning social workers. If your emotional well-being is dependent on financial compensation, definitely do something else.

Understand that your hurt feelings are real, but they aren't always rooted in reality. Sometimes our perceptions are distorted, or we just don't know all the facts. Case in point? The scenario (above) in

1. In mid 2009, the average salary of a youth pastor was $32,156 in North Carolina, $34,541 in Texas, and $36,758 in California (http://www.payscale.com/research/US/Job=Youth_Pastor/Salary/by_State).

which the youth pastor felt hurt because he wasn't asked to perform the wedding of a beloved student. Here's the rest of the story. There's a good reason why he wasn't asked to preside over the ceremony: A few days later the student asked that youth pastor to be his best man!

Understand that the insensitivity of others isn't always intentional. Sometimes people are rude not because they *think ill of you*, but because they *don't think of you at all*. They're too self-absorbed and insecure to consider the feelings of others. Don't take it personally. Their offensive behavior is less a statement about you and more a commentary on them.

Discussion Questions

1. On a scale of 1 to 10, with 1 being "I'm like *Star Trek's* Mr. Spock—I *never* show my emotions" and 10 being "Whatever I'm feeling on the inside will be visible to everyone," how would you rate yourself regarding emotional expression? Why should you be aware of your emotions and how you express them?

2. The late comedian Rodney Dangerfield made a career out of the punch line, "I get no respect." When was the last time you felt like that? What were the circumstances?

3. Which of the opening confessions or scenarios strikes the deepest chord with you? Why?

For Further Study

• Skim the Psalms, especially numbers 1–75, which were mostly written by David. What do you notice about how he dealt with difficult situations and the very powerful emotions they generate?

HOW TO GET RESPECT

• Give respect
• Earn it—act respectably
• Dress appropriately (in other words, professionally)
• Care about your appearance
• Live wisely
• Speak carefully (Proverbs 10:19)
• Love deeply ("love covers over a multitude of sins," 1 Peter 4:8)
• Do the right thing every day (and do it for a long, long time)
• Grow older—wrinkles and gray hair mean something

• Read and ponder Proverbs 29:11 (NIV). This is easy to read but not so easy to do. How does a wise person remain "under control"?

• Read 2 Corinthians. This is the apostle Paul's most personal epistle. It's actually a defense—a response to allegations that Paul's motives were suspect. In it he opens his heart and speaks candidly about the physical and emotional rigors of ministry. Take the time to read it in one sitting.

Avoiding an Avoidable Mess

• Ask God for the grace to let that irritating situation, insensitive comment, inexcusable oversight, or perceived put-down roll off your soul in the same way water rolls right off a duck's back. Don't let it sink in. Shake it off.

• Pray for thicker skin. It's never good to have a *calloused heart* in ministry, but it's important to develop *thick skin*. Ask God to help you learn to deal with criticism and mistreatment in a healthy way.

• Remember what's true. This might be the single most important counsel of all. Whenever you feel punched in the gut, ticked, betrayed, underappreciated, wounded, overwhelmed by sadness, and so forth, resist the urge to just react.

• Find one or two wise, trustworthy souls to whom you can vent. (*Not* students!) Maybe your confidante could be a youth pastor from another church. The two of you could meet for coffee once a week to commiserate and then pray together. Or perhaps it could be an elder in your church or a parent who's really in your corner.

BUILDING A TEAM

Every summer since the early 1980s, a small (and perhaps slightly insane?) group of hard-core bike riders has gathered on the Pacific Coast for the Great American Bike Race (now called the Race Across America). Their goal? To be the first to pedal the entire 3,000-mile journey from coast to coast. You might guess that the effort takes the better part of a month. Guess again. These amazing athletes make the trip in slightly more than *eight days*! That's no typo. The all-time record for the event was set in 1986, when Pete Penseyres cycled 3,107 miles in 8 days, 9 hours, and 47 minutes. Do the math. "Pedaling Pete" averaged—through deserts and over at least two mountain ranges, mind you—15.4 mph, or just a hair under 370 miles a *day*!

I have to be honest: I get worn out at the thought of *driving* 370 miles in one day. How does a cyclist *pedal* from sea to shining sea in barely more than one week? Part of the answer is that these cyclists don't attempt the trip alone. There's a whole team behind each cyclist—and I mean that literally. Riding behind every cyclist in a specially equipped van or RV is a team of three or four friends or family members who play every conceivable role: Cook, strategist, navigator, masseur or masseuse, weather watcher, nurse, trainer, cheerleader, mechanic, and so forth.

What's more, each vehicle is loaded down with supplies—spare tires, parts, and back up bikes; nutritious, high-caloric foods; a bed for quick catnaps; a massage table. Apart from such a support team, even the best cyclists in the world would probably never even make it out of the mountainous West, much less all the way to the East Coast.

In a similar way, youth ministry is a team sport, not an individual pursuit. If you try to minister to students all by yourself, then rest assured that some future youth worker will eventually find your battered soul lying in a ditch by the side of the road, far, far away from the goal.

If I knew then what I know now, I'd spend my first months of youth ministry assembling a top-notch ministry team.

SHARING THE LOAD

When Stacy first asked if we could talk, I (Len) didn't think much about it. I assumed this college student who'd been volunteering with our ministry probably had a question about one of the girls in our youth group. Or maybe she wanted to offer an idea for a meeting or event. So I wasn't prepared for what happened when she showed up at my office. Like a long-tailed cat in a room full of rocking chairs, she was skittish and jumpy, decidedly nervous—fidgeting in her seat, messing with her shoelaces, picking up and replacing the objects on my desk. She made small talk about all kinds of small things until I finally said, "So, Stacy, what's on your mind?"

Wide-eyed, she suddenly froze and stared back at me, "What do you mean?"

"Well, you said you wanted to talk."

"Oh, yeah. That. Well...you see...I've been thinking a lot. And praying. Really praying a lot. And, I guess..." Her voice trailed off as she stared blankly at the picture behind my desk.

Silence.

I waited, watched, and noticed her eyes pooling with tears.

"Stacy, is something wrong?"

Using her fingers like windshield wipers, she tried to sweep away the emotion. "I just think...I probably don't need to work with the youth anymore."

I was flabbergasted. "What? Why would you say that? You're awesome. You're funny. You're sweet. You're walking with God. You have so much to offer. *Those girls need you in their lives*."

Stacy looked up at me, the pooled tears now fully at the mercy of gravity. With a mixture of hurt and frustration, she blurted, "Maybe *they* need me, but obviously *you* don't!"

She buried her face in her hands and shook quietly for 10 or 15 seconds. I felt like the typical idiot guy I was (and am). Should I walk over and pat her on the back? Give her a little hug of encouragement? Crack a joke? Start apologizing? Ask for clarification?

I went with the fifth option. "Stacy, what do you mean I don't need you? Help me understand."

My weeping volunteer suddenly shifted into the anger stage of grief. "Okay, you want to understand. Let me help you. You make this big appeal for volunteers. And so I come to you and tell you I want to work with kids. And not just that, but that I also have a light class load this semester, and that I'd be more than willing to help you in the office. Doing fliers. Making phone calls. Whatever. And you act all excited.

But then you never ask me to do one thing. And so I keep pestering you, 'You want me to come by and do a mailing?' Or 'Hey, I have this great idea for a skit.' Or, 'I was thinking…what if I got some of the girls in my sorority Bible study, and we did a sleepover with the junior high girls and maybe started a Bible study with them?'

"I keep offering. And you keep acting interested. But you never let me do anything. Because it's like *you* have to do *everything*. You have to be the upfront guy—and you have to do everything behind the scenes. Every time I suggest something, you say, 'Yeah, we *definitely* need to think about that.' But nothing ever happens. I never really get a green light. So I just show up at youth meetings and stand around and talk to a few girls. Not that I mind that. I love it. It's great. But I could be doing a lot more than that."

By this time, I was fidgeting with *my* shoelaces. "Stacy, I'm so sorry." I mumbled. "What can I say? I never knew. I feel really bad. Look, tell me the top three or four things you want to do. I'll write them down here, and then we'll get them—and you—scheduled out. I'm sorry. My bad. I've got to unleash you on these girls. We can't afford to have you frustrated and unused. Forgive me for being such a goof, for being so disorganized."

We spent the next 30 minutes talking. Mostly Stacy talked, and I feverishly scribbled notes on a legal pad.

I wish I could tell you that Stacy went on to become the best youth ministry volunteer I've ever worked with. But then—I don't know—I let a few days pass. Then a few weeks. Life got busy. I misplaced my list with all of Stacy's great ideas. Suddenly she quit showing up. Two meetings in a row. Then three. I called and left messages. She never returned my calls. I saw her about four months later in a restaurant. Talk about awkward.

So what was the problem? Was it *disorganization* on my part that kept driving away sharp, qualified volunteers like Stacy? Partly. If you ask for volunteers, then you'd better be prepared to give them a task to do.

But I believe my inability to build a good youth ministry team went deeper. I think it really had more to do with the issue of control. Author and psychologist Henry Cloud says that to one degree or another, we're all control freaks. And I am (or at least I was as a youth pastor) the king of the freaks.

Making fliers, doing announcements, planning meetings, counseling kids, teaching, and leading discussions—if I delegated any of these tasks, if I really relinquished them to the care of another, how could I be sure they'd be done the way I would do them? I couldn't. The truth was that no volunteer could or would do things exactly like I'd do them. So my solution was to keep trying to do everything myself. And the result was a youth ministry volunteer team with a definite "revolving door" feel. Dozens of Stacys, in and then out.

I felt tired and burned out (and lonely) most of the time. And I ended up having an impact on just a handful of kids.

Don't make that same mistake. You can't do it alone. You'll kill yourself or severely limit your effectiveness—or both.

Discussion Questions

1. When have you been in Stacy's situation? What did it feel like? What did you do?

2. How hard is it for you to let others help you? To admit weakness or inability in a certain area? To ask for help? Why, in each case?

3. What are the pros and cons of a team approach to ministry?

4. What character qualities or personality traits are necessary to successfully build a high-functioning, fun ministry team?

For Further Study

• Spend some time reading and reflecting on Exodus 18:13-27. What was Moses doing? What counsel did his pa-in-law give him? What practical applications does this story have on scenarios like the one above?

• Abraham Lincoln once said, "It's amazing how much can be accomplished, if no one cares who gets the credit." Do you agree? What are your deep motivations for youth ministry—credit,

One of my favorite volunteers of all time was Jonathan. As a high school freshman, he sat in the back and never talked to anybody. I'd like to think that my consistent friendliness helped him come out of his shell, but I know now it was the Lord working in his life. By Jonathan's junior year he began interacting with people and offered to create and run PowerPoint for my messages each week (a new technology at the time). He went above and beyond by adding images, sound effects, animation, transitions, and more. By the time he started college, though, he was bored with that and asked if he could join the high school volunteer staff. And not long after that, he asked if he could teach.

Teach? Really? Is this the same Jonathan who wouldn't speak to people four years ago? Now he was on my staff and asking if he could speak in front of the whole youth group. So I told him I'd help him prepare and give him a chance.

It was the most uncomfortable presentation I've ever heard. Jonathan cried through the whole message. Every time he started talking about Jesus, he burst into tears. I kept thinking that I should go up, pat him on the back, tell him "thanks for trying," and save him further humiliation by telling him to sit down. But I let him stumble through it.

Honestly, I can't remember anything specific he talked about. (Most of it was garbled by all the phlegm.) But I do remember the response afterward. Kids were overwhelmed by Jonathan's courage, and they thanked him for sharing his heart.

Soon after that, he spoke to the group again. He cried through just half of it that time. And the third time he spoke to them, he cried only once. After that, he never had a problem with his confidence.

Recently, Jonathan graduated from college, and he's preparing to serve in Venezuela as a full-time missionary. Now he's teaching God's Word confidently—and not only in English, but in Spanish as well!

Through watching Jonathan mature in his faith, I learned that God can and will use anybody who's willing to serve. And I learned to be patient. Maturity doesn't happen overnight. We learn from our experiences (mostly from our failures), and God helps us grow through every opportunity as long as we are faithful to him.
—J. T. Bean

applause, strokes, praise, God's glory, the spiritual life and growth of teenagers, pay, what?

Avoiding an Avoidable Mess

• With support from a trusted friend who knows you well, do a personal inventory. What are your strengths—the things you do best? What are your weaknesses or holes—the abilities God has not given to you? The more time you spend answering these two questions, the closer you'll be to building a killer youth ministry.

• If you're a full-time youth director or pastor, track your use of time. How much time do you spend doing what volunteers could do?

• Ask yourself what the most pressing needs are in your existing youth ministry. Where does your ministry need teachers, counselors, helpers, cooks, discussion leaders, chaperones, drivers, and so forth? Identify existing holes and quantify how many volunteer slots you have.

BAD MINISTRY MATH

Seventy-seven percent of all youth pastors confess that they routinely worry about how many kids attend (or don't attend) their stuff. And, as the old joke goes, the other 23 percent are liars.

I (Len) cannot tell a lie. I've *always* noticed empty chairs. Even when I don't actually write down the figures, I mentally keep track of numbers, averages. I mean, when you get right down to it, don't people vote with their feet?

One group that I had years ago began in the spring with two students at a burger bash. Yep, two. By the fall, we were up to 12 or 15 attenders. A year later, we had a lively group of 50 or 60. And the next year we were drawing 150 students to our midweek meeting. Hey, when a group grows in quantity like that, *something* is going on, right? Either God is at work or the number of cute girls is reaching critical mass, thereby attracting more and more cool guys. But *something's* happening, right?

Numbers. They can make leaders of small, struggling groups defensive: Jesus told us to *feed* his sheep. He never called us to *count* them. Besides, he started with 12 and ended with 11. And *he* was the Son of God! If numbers are all God cares about, then how come every time Jesus started drawing a crowd, he purposely said or did something to cause the majority of folks to walk away?

Attendance figures can make leaders of blowing and growing groups cocky: "Yeah, well, last time *I* checked, there's also a whole book of the Bible called 'Numbers.' Obviously, God keeps records. And why? Because each number represents an actual person who matters to God. So the more numbers we have, the more hearts we're impacting! It's the nature of how healthy things grow, right?"

And on and on it goes.

I don't know the answer—or even if there is an answer—to the age-old numbers debate, but I've learned this: A youth ministry *team* can touch way more lives than *one* solitary youth worker. Maybe that's why Jesus gathered a group of followers who, after they were trained, were instructed to go out and gather other followers.

It's the *multiplication* model of ministry versus the simple *addition* model. Consider this: If you pour yourself into 10 kids a year and do youth ministry for a decade, then you'll end up deeply impacting 100 kids (10 +10 +10 +10 +10 +10 +10 +10 +10 +10 = 100). And, as a bonus, you'll probably set a denominational record for the longest youth worker tenure. You might even get a bonus!

On the other hand, if you gather and train 10 new youth *volunteers* a year (adults, collegians, plus a couple of older, more mature youth) and

Sure, sure, we want to reach as many kids as possible. Yes, we're compelled by Christ to take the gospel to students. But nowhere in Scripture do we get any inclination that God prefers a group of 700 kids over a group of eight. In fact, most of the stuff I find in the Bible seems to point just the other way: God wanted Gideon to have less men in his army; God sent Joshua to Jericho without large numbers or weapons; David got in big-time trouble for counting his troops. Nothing will burn you out faster than being small and striving for large. Nothing will lead you to pride faster than having a large group and focusing on that fact. Check out the story of Uzziah (2 Chronicles 26) if you need to know the result of pride.

—Mark Oestreicher

I thought bigger was better. It's part of our culture to think this way. I put this in my ministry dreams. Bigger staff numbers and organization were priorities when I first had the opportunity to determine ministry goals. In a few years, the organization I'd built crumbled. They always do. The core of ministry is relationships to build in the lives of others. It was a "Duh-hhhhhh" moment, but this is what Jesus did. He touched all that followed him. His primary focus was the lives of 12 men.

—*Tom Morris*

they in turn each pour themselves into a bunch of kids, then over a 10-year time period that ministry will impact upwards of 1,000 kids. The "Jethro Principle" (see Exodus 18:21), adapted for ministry, says that at most, a person can adequately care for about 10 others. Want a vibrant youth group of 200 students? That will take approximately 20 committed volunteers.

Each youth leader has to ask: *Do I simply want big numbers of teenagers at my weekly events—or do I want to see students meet Christ and have their lives changed in significant, eternal ways?* I'll go out on a limb and predict that you want substance, not flash. You want long-term maturity and stability in your students, not short-term popularity of your youth activities.

So make the conscious choice to involve others. Recruit volunteers. Help them discover and use their God-given abilities for ministry. Then step back and let them shine. Make it your goal to see your volunteers blossom. As you "give away" the ministry, you'll get more than you ever imagined. More students. More changed lives. More ministry health and success. More personal satisfaction. More glory for God.

Discussion Questions

1. What, if anything, can we learn from numbers, attendance figures, and counting the warm bodies at our ministry events?

2. How much of your self-worth and happiness in ministry is tied to the number of kids who show up at your youth ministry functions? Why?

3. What do you think of the so-called Jethro Principle (that one person can adequately care for about 10 others)? Is it valid? Why or why not?

For Further Study

• Spend some time reading and reflecting on 2 Timothy 2:2. In his final letter, Paul challenged his young protégé Timothy with the principle of ministry multiplication. What would this look like in down-to-earth, concrete terms in *your* life and ministry?

• Ponder Matthew 4:18-22. What is significant about the fact that when Jesus first called his followers, he laid out the expectation that they'd become ministers themselves?

Avoiding an Avoidable Mess

• Talk with your ministry supervisor (your senior pastor or organizational director) about expectations for your group.

• Gather three or four ministry colleagues and have a discussion about the meaning of numbers. You probably won't agree on what high (or low) attendance means or signifies. But you'll sharpen one another's thinking.

• Ask God for the wisdom and grace to take the long view. Remember that packing a room full of kids each week does little good if only a few of those adolescents are still walking with God five years later.

STAFFING IN LIGHT OF YOUR WEAKNESSES

Consider how this veteran youth worker (who prefers to stay anonymous) describes the progression of youth leaders who've served in his congregation in recent years:

> Over the last 10 to 12 years, the youth leaders at our church have covered the spectrum. We once had a youth pastor who was radically outreach-oriented, always engaging the kids in edgy, inner-city ministry to the "least of these." He really lived out the gospel, and our group became extremely mission-minded during his tenure. It was neat to watch. He wasn't the most scintillating youth *speaker* ever. For instance, he once gave a long, rambling talk that utilized the nine-point acronym D-R-A-M-A-M-I-N-E (I'm not making this up.) But it didn't matter. The students and volunteer leaders loved him deeply.
>
> The next guy we hired was quieter and steadier. Much more low-key, more focused on building deep relationships. That was his great strength. He was a natural counselor, connecting with kids one-on-one

and getting them to open up. Our youth group was much smaller then, but it was tight-knit.

When he left, we hired a kid-magnet, life-of-the-party guy who could just take over a room. He was off-the-charts fun and social. He never did completely win over the fans of his calmer predecessor, but he attracted a whole new group of kids, including lots of loud, unchurched kids.

I guess we discovered that a group will tend to take on its leader's personality. So if you have a bookish and thoughtful guy, you'll mostly attract those kinds of quieter kids. To keep the group from becoming unbalanced, you'll need additional leaders and volunteers with other personality types and gifts.

We recently did a survey to find out what our students and their parents are looking for (or hoping for) in our next youth pastor. When we compiled our responses, it was like that old joke—all we want is everything! Someone who's young and energetic (but also extremely wise!), married (but with loads of free time!), a gifted counselor and evangelist and Bible teacher and visionary and kid magnet and spiritual director and team builder. We'd like someone who is social *and* serious *and* deep *and* experienced *and* service-minded. I know, I know—it sounds like what we really want is *Jesus*. Or at least some kind of "Super Youth Pastor" who doesn't exist. But hey, why not go for the moon? Ephesians 3:20, right?

I'm sure what will eventually happen is exactly what's happened in the past. The person we hire will have a certain personality type, plus a handful of unique, God-given abilities and passions. He or she will also have certain quirks and flaws and disinterests, not to mention some obvious God-ordained lacks. And we'll just have to staff in light of those weaknesses. If our choice isn't very adept at administration, then we'll need to address that deficiency with volunteers. If our new leader is naturally drawn to the more outgoing kids, then we'll need to recruit some different helper types who tend to notice the quieter students.

Whoever we get will need a team of talented and committed folks supporting him or her. That's our goal.

A few years ago, our (Dave) director of student ministries was getting flak from both sides. One well-respected church member with two daughters in the youth group was vocal about his disappointment with the ministry. He thought it needed to be deeper—fewer games and more serious Bible study. Another sharp, young dad who had a son in the group told me, "Bill needs to lighten up. I think he needs a comedian to open the meetings for him." (He was serious.)

While I don't think Bill would ever be able to satisfy both of those fathers, his dilemma points to a reality we all face: The ministries we lead will reflect who we are—our personalities, interests, and gifts. And that's fine. But we need to remember that lots of kids—a wide variety of them—need Christ, and we must enlist the help of all types of leaders to reach them.

Discussion Questions

1. How would the people who know you best describe you? What are your strengths and limitations?

2. Do you know your spiritual gifts? Do you know your God-given abilities for serving Christ's church?

3. What skills do you lack that you wish you had?

4. What types of students or kinds of kids (for example, jocks, preps, and so on) are currently involved in your church or youth group or parachurch ministry? What kinds of teenagers do you feel the most comfortable working with? How about the least comfortable? Why?

For Further Study

• Spend some time carefully reading the great spiritual gift chapter—1 Corinthians 12. Why such God-ordained diversity? How does the church, as God designed it, resemble a symphony orchestra, a football team, or a combustion engine?

• Meditate on Colossians 4:7-18. *Paul's* ministry team was a hodge-podge of assorted souls. Why would *Luke* have been a good colleague for Paul? (Note: Paul was a Jewish rabbi; Luke was a Gentile doctor.)

Avoiding an Avoidable Mess

• Getting a wide assortment of *personality types* on your youth ministry team is necessary for success.

• If you live in a college town, then drop to your knees right now and thank the good Lord for the mother lode of potential volunteer talent living right up the street. In and around the various campus ministries, it's likely that you'll find a number of sharp, God-loving students who've been discipled in their faith or worked at Christian camps and have an interest in working with youth. Don't make the mistake, however, of thinking that only the most studly (and spiritual) frat guys and the most gorgeous (and godly) sorority girls can really connect with high school students. It takes all kinds.

EFFECTIVE RECRUITING

Okay, by now you're realizing the insanity of trying to do youth ministry alone. You're aware of your strengths and weaknesses, and you're committed to compensating for your shortcomings by finding a team of volunteers with strengths you don't possess. Perfect.

Now you actually have to start recruiting. But if you're like most folks, then you probably don't feel that recruiting is your strong suit. You know how busy people are, and you feel guilty asking them to add one more thing to their lives (even a really important thing like youth ministry).

You have a couple of options. You could pray like crazy that God will drop a willing volunteer into your life—someone who loves you and is a huge fan of the youth group, a charming persuasive soul who loves talking on the phone and enjoys nothing more than recruiting others to serve in eternally worthy causes. Or you could be a little more in touch with reality and see this moment as a prime opportunity to stretch your own faith while you watch God bring together your youth ministry dream team.

Don't wait around and depend solely on prayer! Who was it that said, "Pray like everything depends on God and work like everything depends on you"? That's good advice.

Grab your cell phone and start praying *while* you punch the numbers. See what God does.

As you search for volunteers, don't fall into the trap of believing that young adults are always the best people to work with teenagers. That's a common misconception throughout the church, and it may also be your assumption—especially if you're under 25 years of age. Somewhere we got the idea that *younger* adults relate to kids far better than older ones do.

Certainly, that idea has some truth. And young adults can make great youth workers. Since they're often unmarried and without children of their own, young adults tend to have more flexible schedules and tons of energy. They tend to be more in tune with youth culture, and they have the added advantage of still remembering (often vividly) what being a teenager is like.

But older workers have distinct advantages as well. They bring life experience, maturity, and wisdom. And those who have children can relate well to other parents.

One veteran youth worker puts it this way:

As I got older and continued to work with kids, my ministry approach changed. The first changes I noticed were physical—I couldn't run as hard or as long with them as I did right out of college. And after I got married, I had another person to consider as I arranged my schedule. When children came, they brought a whole new set of challenges. But through the years I've seen my ministry *deepen*. My ability to communicate and to build friendships with kids hasn't lessened; in fact, it's probably gotten stronger. And I find that I have much more to say based on how I've applied Scripture and how I've seen God work in my life.

Hopefully you're committed to developing a team approach to ministry. In other words, you're not to do it all yourself. Team ministry will provide the much-needed diversity of gender, age, life experience, and ethnic background.

Students may see a young adult leader as an older brother or sister, or a cool older friend. A 30-year-old leader may be seen as a surrogate aunt or uncle. Someone a bit older can become a secondary parent figure (increasingly important with the current breakdown of the family). And grandparents bring their own strengths, too.

Discussion Questions

1. How are you when it comes to recruiting? Do you like it, hate it, or just tolerate it? How effective are you at doing it?

2. What are the characteristics of good recruiting? What are some of the tangible qualities and intangible elements that attract a person to be part of a team?

3. Think back on the fruitful youth ministries you've seen or been a part of. Who were some of the unheralded team members who made those groups a success? What roles did they play?

For Further Study

• Read and ponder Jesus' statement in Matthew 16:18—"*I will build my church.*" What are the implications of this claim for your youth ministry? For your effort to recruit a youth ministry team? How does this promise affect the pressure you're feeling?

• Read Psalm 33:16-18.

Avoiding an Avoidable Mess

Recruiting Reminders
- Recruit broadly
- Put together a youth group advisory team or parent council
- Recruit outside the box
- Cast the vision
- Make the "ask"
- Give people the freedom to say "no"
- Let people try before they buy
- Trust the sovereignty of God

APPRECIATING YOUR COWORKERS

This well-seasoned youth worker offers a great reminder about the importance of making your team feel valued:

> Once upon a time, I ministered to teens full time as part of a parachurch organization. I very much enjoyed what I was doing, and I loved the people I worked alongside. But even though I worked really hard and did my job with excellence, my pay was shockingly low. To make matters worse, my boss rarely spoke to me. He didn't rag on me (I was thankful for that!), but he also didn't give me any words of gratitude or appreciation. At times I felt taken for granted. Sometimes I felt invisible.
>
> After several years—and I think after getting wind of the fact that I was getting restless and considering leaving—my ministry director asked another staff member (who outranked me) to take me to dinner at a fancy, overpriced restaurant.
>
> I gladly would have traded that $200 meal for an occasional note or phone call. Maybe if I'd felt valued, I'd have worked there longer. I know this much—the experience marked me in a deep way. I resolved that I would always try to make sure my coworkers, helpers, volunteers, and interns felt appreciated.

The ministry is tough. And even though we don't do ministry in order to get something, when we get *nothing,* it's hard to stay motivated for long.

How can we encourage and appreciate volunteers? Here are some ideas for recognizing volunteers and keeping them motivated:

Email/text messages: Even if you have two left thumbs, how long does it take to compose a short note that says: "Hey, I can't tell you how glad I am that you're on our team. You add *so much.* What would I do without you?" Or just, "Thnx 4 wrkng w/ students!"

Written cards: Keep some postcards on hand (already stamped). You can dash off two or three in 10 minutes' time while you're on hold, standing in line, or waiting for a meeting to begin. A card shows a bit more effort and is much more special than an email. Electronic messages usually get deleted, but a sincere handwritten note is often tucked away in a Bible or journal and reread multiple times.

Phone calls: Put everyone in your cell phone directory and get in the habit of making quick calls. "What's up? Hey, I was just thinking about you and thanking God for you!"

Verbal affirmation: Look your people in the eyes and speak from your heart. "Wow! You did that *really* well; God has really gifted you!" Or bring them up in front of the larger group and make a fuss over them.

Touch: A pat on the back, a hug (side by side, an arm around the shoulder, and a squeeze), or a high-five. These little physical touches can communicate gratitude and affection like nothing else.

Thoughtful, inexpensive gifts: Candy bars, packs of gum, framed pictures, homemade cookies, little paperback books you buy in bulk—the list is endless. A friend in ministry does something like this at least monthly for her volunteers, and they appreciate being appreciated. Little things have a big impact.

Dinners: Take a couple of volunteers at a time to eat at Subway or Chili's, your treat. (Unless you work at Bill Gates Memorial Bible Church, you'll probably need to budget for this, too.)

Remember birthdays and anniversaries: At least email or text. Better yet, call. Special days deserve special acknowledgments.

Volunteer of the Month bulletin boards: Someone has wisely said, "You cultivate what you celebrate"—meaning, if you make a big deal out of those who do volunteer, you just might get more volunteers!

Mentions in the church newsletter: Years ago, our church dumped its old-fashioned snail-mail monthly newsletter and went to a weekly e-letter. One of the most popular features of our new communiqué is a brief interview with a volunteer. These ministry spotlights are always fun, surprising, and encouraging.

Recognition in churchwide gatherings: Make them stand up. Clap for 'em. Make them come forward. Even when people act embarrassed by such attention, something within them appreciates being recognized.

Annual banquets: We've had fancy appreciation dinners with seafood gumbo and turtle soup. We've had catered affairs at local restaurants. Memorable barbecues (with line dancing). Fish fries. Wild game nights. Crawfish boils with Cajun music. Whatever the theme or menu, the point is to gather volunteer workers (and their spouses or dates) and celebrate what God has done.

Discussion Questions

1. When have you been in a situation where you felt unappreciated? Describe what happened and how you felt.

2. In light of the example given by Jesus in Luke 17:7-10, is it wrong for servants of Christ to *want* to be valued and appreciated? To *expect* it? To *demand* it?

3. Why is it a good idea to say "thank you" to our volunteers in a variety of ways?

For Further Study

• Spend some time reflecting on Romans 12:10 (ESV) and what it means to "outdo one another in showing honor."

• Meditate on Romans 16:1-16. Note how Paul acknowledged, appreciated, and affirmed his cohorts in the gospel.

Avoiding an Avoidable Mess

• Check out the book *The Heart of the Five Love Languages* (Northfield Publishing, 2007). Author Gary Chapman makes a compelling case that the way to someone's heart is via one of five possible "love languages": Physical touch, words of affirmation, quality time, acts of service, or tangible gifts. This a helpful concept for not only dealing with kids, but also volunteers. Affirming someone with that person's preferred love language multiplies its effectiveness.

• Create a birthday and anniversary list or calendar so you don't miss important days.

RELATIONSHIPS WITH KIDS

Thinking back, way back, to your days in junior high and high school—who were your favorite teachers? Why? Next, consider your coaches, music or drama directors, and club sponsors—which ones evoke good memories? And if you grew up in church, include your Sunday school teachers, pastors, and youth leaders in the mix. Who affected you the most? Why?

Certainly we might recall adults who led an important learning event or activity—perhaps a field trip, guest lecture, or "aha!" moment in class or on the field. But most of us will remember those caring adults with whom we had a relationship—friendship even—men and women who cared about us. Those were the life changers.

So we shouldn't be surprised that relationships with teenagers play such a vital role in effective youth ministry. Most youth leaders know that, of course; but programs and plans and procedures can push us away from students and even out of the picture. Our games can be great fun, our lessons profound, and our wrap-ups moving, but the relationships we form with individual students will make the greatest difference.

If I knew then what I know now, I would have invested most of my time in building relationships with kids—building my life into them.

A WORLD OF HURT

Take a look at a group of students hanging out at a game or other school activity or in the youth lounge before the meeting. You'll see animated conversations and interesting facial expressions with some students trying hard to be cool and others hoping to fit in. You could easily assume that, at least for these students, life is good.

Steven Brown says that when he preaches, he assumes that 75 percent of the congregation is hurting. Behind the nice clothes, pious expressions, and plastered smiles, individuals are in pain, struggling.

Our students are no different. Behind every face and every smile lies drama. It's always been that way, of course. But these days, in addition to the normal adolescent issues—self-doubt, guilt, nagging questions, pulsing sexuality, and aching loneliness—many kids are also struggling with major issues, such as substance abuse, depression, and physical or sexual abuse.

We need to assume that stuff is going on inside them, that private intense battles are being waged daily, that students—our students—are hurting. Therefore, since we know the pain is real and we love these young people, we need to be proactive—spending time with individual students, asking them questions, talking about their interests, and, most importantly, listening to them.

I (Dave) remember sitting at a corner table in the high school cafeteria with a junior girl who'd asked to have an "appointment" with me. I made small talk about the school, the cafeteria food, and the big game. Then, as I paused for a breath, she said something like, "What I really wanted to talk about..." and proceeded to open up about *her* life and *her* issues. What a wake-up call—I had to be *interrupted* to listen to this girl!

Listening may be the most difficult part of building relationships with teenagers because our conversations with them will be liberally sprinkled with their versions of opposite-sex dramas, issues with teachers, theories about life—and occasional rants. We'll want to interrupt—to set them straight, to correct their bad theology, or to offer advice. But often our best response is silence—simply listening and building trust, thereby deepening the relationship.

Teenagers—hurting teenagers—need someone who hears, who understands, who cares.

Discussion Questions

1. When you were a teenager, what secret burdens did you carry?

On a Sunday evening, a special time was given to the kids in our youth group to share a significant experience they'd had during the past year of youth ministry. I was sure they'd talk about the National Convention in Washington, the ski trip to Colorado, the mission trip to Honduras, the tremendous weekly youth meetings we'd had with all the skits, music, and, of course, spiritual challenges. And, yes, a number of students did mention these and other events.

But one young man, Scott, who was a leader in our group stood to speak: "I've enjoyed this year with all the activities of our youth group. But my best experience was spending two days with Jim in an unair-conditioned cargo van picking up those throw-out Christmas trees a week after Christmas. You remember the 200 we burned at our annual New Year's bonfire? They were sticky and sappy, but that was okay. What was great was we just talked and laughed. We shared our lives and our hearts and listened to each other.

It wasn't planned. There was no script—just two guys working together, being buddies for two great days. What made it great was the relationship we formed in that van. It wasn't a student and a leader—it was just two guys. It wasn't a big activity—it was just being together without anything planned. That was my best experience of the youth ministry year for me."
—*Jim Green*

2. What hidden hurts might the students in your group have? How do you know?

3. Listening is called "the language of love." Why?

4. What can you do to be a better listener?

For Further Study

• Identify your closest relationships (spouse, good friend, small group, and so on) and think about what built those relationships. Make a list. It may include things like these: We have lot in common; we spend time together; she affirms me and makes me feel special; he accepts me; she listens to me without judging; and so forth. Consider how you can take those same actions with your students to build relationships with them.

• Reread 1 Corinthians 13, thinking of how you relate to specific students in love.

Try a listening experiment. For a whole day, work at looking people in the eye and focusing on what they're saying. Refuse to interrupt them.

Avoiding an Avoidable Mess

• Get a counseling book (such as *At Risk: Bringing Hope to Hurting Teenagers* by Scott Larson, *Helping the Struggling Adolescent* by Dr. Les Parrott III, or *The Youth Worker's Guide to Helping Teenagers in Crisis* by Rich Van Pelt and Jim Hancock) and look for signals or signs of pain and hurt in teenagers.

• Keep a prayer list with specific needs for specific students. Pray regularly for these kids.

• Don't be afraid to check in with individual students and ask how they're *really* doing. Then listen when they begin to open up.

FRIEND OR AUTHORITY FIGURE?

Early in my (Dave) ministry, our local Campus Life chapter rented a camp in Wisconsin for a week one summer and filled just about every available space with high school students. I was excited about the guys from my two schools—a bunch of football players and their buddies—and I roomed with some of them in one of the cabins. I'd worked hard at building friendships with these guys—watching their practices, working out with them, hanging out one-on-one, and making sure they were welcome and involved in our club meetings. So I assumed I could parlay those friendships into gaining their full cooperation, especially at night.

What a mistake!

As soon as the lights went out, the guys went crazy—talking and then yelling, throwing stuff around the room, making gross comments—typical stuff for adolescent athletes. And I didn't know what to do. I turned on the lights and tried to talk them out of it with a brief speech using the "Hey, guys, we're friends" approach.

It didn't work. Every time the lights went out, chaos ensued.

And I found myself becoming furious with them. Rather than risk ruining the friendships and blowing all my relationship-building efforts by yelling at them or calling them jerks, I left the building.

That wasn't one of my better moments in youth ministry. I didn't see how I could be the authority and a friend at the same time.

Most young youth workers face this dilemma, especially those who believe strongly in relational youth ministry. I wish I'd known then what I know now: We can be friends *and* in charge (and enforce the limits and rules) at the same time.

When I was in seminary, I remember hearing Bill Starr, the president of Young Life, tell us

At first I had to speak the lingo, play guitar, and throw around youth culture references. That was me—the funky-fresh youth-meister.

To be painfully honest, I still struggle with this misconception. And my probability of successfully pulling off "cool" is decreasing by the day. But like many youth workers, I want kids to think I'm cool. And it's easy to fall into the false thinking that being cool increases ministry effectiveness. Not exactly.

Matt was a volunteer youth worker at my last church. Matt is cool. Actually, Matt is quite possibly the single biggest geek you'd ever meet. He's just wrapping up a Ph.D. in theoretical chemistry. It's not even real chemistry. They use computers to play what-if games about compounds and molecules. He's a full-on pocket-protector-wearing, plaid-pants-with-a-striped-shirt, rhythm-deficient, stereotypical dweeb. And he's one of the most effective youth workers I've ever met. He reaches kids I'd never reach. And I don't mean he's only good with computer-geek future theoretical chemists. He loves on teens and sticks with them, and he's unapologetically himself. Students love him, and they respect his authenticity.

Put-on hipness might get you some initial attention with students, but it won't take you very far. God's best gift to your ministry is you. And your best programming tool is you. Be yourself.

—Mark Oestreicher

The role of the youth worker is not to be a buddy or a pal. If you're hanging out with teenagers all the time and see them as peers and best friends, then something is wrong with you, and you shouldn't be in youth ministry! Sure, you'll befriend kids. But you're their leader, and that defines you as a different kind of friend. Yes, you'll hang out and talk about things other than Jesus. But your relationships with students, as chummy as they may seem at times, need to maintain the foundational understanding that your reason for hanging is not to be a pal; it's to have a spiritual impact on their lives.

—Mark Oestreicher

during chapel that students don't need another "teenager" as a youth leader. They need *adults* acting like *adults* who will come alongside them and listen, empathize, understand, offer counsel, guide, and, in short, be their friend. And this was from the folks who practically invented relational youth ministry!

Don't fall into the trap of believing you need to be one of the guys (or gals) by adopting the clothing styles, musical tastes, and clichés your students use. If those are genuine places where you connect with kids, then that's fine. But what's important is to *be yourself*. Kids don't need another kid—they need you, a mature adult who comes to the situation with experience and wisdom.

One YFC staff member was trying so hard to be liked by a group of guys that he suggested that a great prank would be to let the air out of the tires of the school buses. He got fired. Being an adult means being responsible in all areas. We'll talk more about this when we discuss safety issues in chapter 11.

Now back to my camp story: I quickly learned that I had to set limits, explaining firmly and quietly the rules and the consequences for breaking them. You know what? The guys respected that—they understood and responded well. In fact, most of them had coaches they respected and liked who did the same.

Discussion Questions

1. Think back to coaches, teachers, and other adult leaders whom you respected and admired. Why did you feel close to them? What limits did they set, and how did they enforce them? What can you learn from their approaches that will help you build responsible relationships with students?

2. When have you been torn between being a buddy and being an authority figure? What happened? What do you wish you'd done differently?

3. What do you think being a teenager's adult friend means?

For Further Study

• Read *When Church Kids Go Bad: How to Love and Work with Rude, Obnoxious, and Apathetic Students* by Les Christie, noting especially chapters 6 and 7.

• Get a copy of *The Grace and Truth Paradox: Responding with Christlike Balance* by Randy Alcorn. Use this as a discussion starter for your staff on how to balance loving kids to Christ, while at the same time telling them the truth.

Avoiding an Avoidable Mess

• Teenagers need limits, especially early adolescents and younger. The limits (rules and expectations) provide a sense of security and well-being. Think about the limits you have with your group, with individual students, in your meetings, and at special events. How are you communicating those limits in love?

• If you're sponsoring a retreat, camp, or high-adventure experience, think through how you'll communicate the rules beforehand and how you'll enforce them during the event. You may want to practice your "rules speech."

CONFRONTATION

Following on the heels of the friend versus authority figure dilemma is the issue of confrontation. Inevitably, in youth ministry occasions will arise when we have to say, "Stop!" "No!" "You're way out of line!" or something

Matt was a junior high kid who never stopped talking. During my Bible lesson, he'd talk as much as I did and at only a slightly lesser volume! I made numerous futile attempts to shut him up. I'd give him the "evil eye." I'd stop speaking and wait until he quieted down, assuming that would embarrass him into submission. I'd lecture the entire group about "respecting God's Word" in the hopes that guilt would overwhelm him toward repentance. I'd sit one of our adult leaders directly behind him to discreetly express our disapproval with a gentle hand on his shoulder. I'd even make him my special target during the dodgeball game that followed lesson time. (Honestly, hasn't every youth pastor taken out his or her frustrations on a junior high antagonist via dodgeball?) But nothing deterred Matt from being a disruptive force of evil.

Then one night I got an idea—bribery! I approached Matt with an offer he couldn't refuse. If he remained perfectly quiet during my lesson, I'd buy him a Mountain Dew afterward. Yeah, sugar and caffeine weren't exactly what he needed, but I was desperate. He enthusiastically agreed to the deal. To my great satisfaction, he went the entire 20 minutes without talking. As I handed him his well-earned can of pop, I placed my arm around him and said, "I'm proud of you Matt! Congratulations! Enjoy your pop! But, know this: You just proved to me that you can be quiet if you want to be. From now on I expect you not to talk while I'm talking." I went on to express my appreciation for his frenetic energy level and his potential leadership qualities in our group. I made it clear that I cared about him and that I was looking to him to set the example for his friends.

The results? Though not perfect, Matt improved greatly and would actually have a look of pride on his face as he made a conscious effort to keep his mouth shut! I learned to deal one-on-one with teens that are chronic discipline problems, doing so in private while casting a new vision for them regarding their behavior and their influence in our group. As corny as it might sound, most students want to be believed in and will often rise to the level of our expectations. Strategic bribery seems to be effective, too.

—*Dave Corlew*

similar. An-eighth grade boy continues to disrupt the group by making strange noises. A sophomore girl can't stop talking to her friends, even during a serious talk. A junior guy pokes or pinches the guys sitting around him, causing them to jump and yelp. And much worse.

So how, exactly, do we confront such troublesome behavior without destroying any semblance of the friendship we've built? While this list isn't exhaustive, here are a few principles gleaned from those who've been through it.

Keep it private. One of the worst things we can do is embarrass teenagers in front of their friends. Calling out a student in a meeting, especially with sarcasm or anger, is almost always a very bad idea. That public confrontation probably won't correct the problem, and it certainly will harm the relationship.

Of course, if an action could cause someone harm—either the offender or someone else—then we'll have to step in immediately and take action. But in situations where such intervention isn't necessary, a much better approach would be to get with the offender one-on-one and explain the rules and why breaking them is a problem. We can explain the consequences of future offenses as well.

Keep it serious. Sometimes we may be so afraid of confrontation that we joke about the issue and the offense. If we "confront" in this way, then students won't take us seriously, and we shouldn't be surprised if wrong behavior continues.

If a member of the group has been disruptive or disrespectful or has ignored an important guideline or rule, then we should explain—in all seriousness—the guideline or rule, the reasons for it, and the expectation of compliance.

Keep it real. This means communicating sincerely and with empathy, letting the individual know we understand a bit about her motives and feelings. And it might include sharing our personal experiences of "getting in trouble" at church or in school. The student should know we don't believe she is a terrible or weird person.

This also means being realistic about our rules and the consequences for breaking them. We need to be sure the punishment for an infraction fits the crime—and that we actually can and will do what we threaten to do.

I (Dave) once had to miss a Campus Life/JV meeting at our local middle school. The next day, my coleader, a shop teacher named Steve, explained that he'd had to tell two boys they couldn't come to our next two meetings because of the way they'd acted that day. I was shocked. I was thinking those guys probably would never return, and they were exactly the kind of students we were trying to reach.

Although I didn't say what I was thinking, Steve must have read my mind. He explained that he didn't think we should jeopardize the whole group because of the actions of those two.

He was right. And those two boys did return once their "suspension" ended.

If we want kids to respect our rules, then we need to follow through and enforce the threatened consequences. If we don't—if we continually let it slide—then we'll find it even more difficult the next time we try to enforce the rules.

At times, confronting troublesome behavior will be necessary. But if it's done right, it doesn't have to hurt a relationship.

But what about spiritual confrontation? Some Christians believe it's their duty, their calling, to confront individuals about their sins and their need of the Savior. While the motives are admirable, the tactics are not. Usually people are turned off and turned away from that kind of aggressive, in-your-face approach.

Similarly, some youth leaders seem to look for specific sins to condemn, whether it's in a group setting or one-on-one. And they usually end up with very small youth groups.

Conversely, however, some Christians soft-pedal the gospel so much that they never get around to the sin part and the reason for Christ's death on the cross. In an effort to get close to kids, they forget why they're in the ministry.

One youth minister shares:

Years ago, I was talking with a youth director from a church across town. I believed strongly in relational evangelism, which involved getting to know kids and "winning the right to be heard." This other guy's philosophy seemed to be to declare the truth boldly, to take a much more

I once thought that if I wiggled and manipulated my way into the closest confidence of students, I'd be able to address their deepest and darkest sins. The flaw in this thinking wasn't in my ability to find out about their deepest and darkest sins. The flaw was in thinking this was good ministry.

Let's face it. I was trying to be the Holy Spirit! How stupid is that? I continue to meet 30- and 40-year-old youth workers still laboring under the false assumption that their job is to convict students of sin. Let's leave God's work to God.

Not that you shouldn't confront sin. You should. But that's not your primary role.
—*Mark Oestreicher*

aggressive approach to witnessing. So in our conversation that day, I challenged him: "When are you going to stop yelling and start listening—to stop driving by those campuses and spend time there getting to know real, hurting teenagers?" And so on.

He seemed to take it in. But then he said, "When are you going to have the courage to tell kids the truth about Jesus?" And I had to admit that he had a point. Often I was so concerned about turning someone off about Christ (actually about me), that I wouldn't say anything at all. I found walking across those relational bridges I'd built to be quite difficult. I was afraid of losing their friendship.
—*[Anonymous]*

So in this discussion of building relationships with students, we must understand our holy obligation to tell them the truth—about sin, about heaven and hell, about Jesus, and about what to expect as a follower of Christ. We share these truths in love.

Discussion Questions

1. Why are some kids so disruptive? Why do some seem to always break the rules?

2. What students do you have the most difficulty confronting about their behavior? Why them?

3. When have you lost your cool with a group or individual? What happened to your relationship with them? What did you do to get it back on track?

4. Why do kids need limits (discipline, rules for behavior, standards)? What will you do to enforce those limits?

For Further Study
• Read chapters 8 and 10 of *When Church Kids Go Bad: How to Love and Work with Rude, Obnoxious, and Apathetic Students* by Les Christie.

• Reflect on Proverbs 27:6, 17. Consider how those principles apply to loving confrontations with students.

• Read chapter 11, "Spitballs and Pitfalls," of *Dave's Complete Guide to Junior High Ministry* by Dave Veerman (available electronically through www.WordSearchBible.com).

Avoiding an Avoidable Mess
• If you've recently confronted a student the wrong way, speak with that student privately and express regret, asking for that person's forgiveness. Let the young person know you care for him specifically, as well as for the whole group, and you want everyone to feel welcome and accepted.

• With your staff, role-play possible confrontation scenarios and how you, and they, should handle such situations.

KEEPING SECRETS
Remember in middle school when you told your best friend how you felt about that certain someone of the opposite sex? You swore that friend to secrecy, yet a few days later the news was all over school—and you were embarrassed and angry.

Just a couple of experiences like that can make us reluctant to open up to others, to share our true feelings, ideas, insecurities, desires, disappointments, and dreams. To this day you may find it difficult to open up to others for fear of being hurt again.

Over a Diet Coke one afternoon, Mollie began to open up. At first we talked about her friends. Then she explained some of her recent reactions to what we'd been discussing in youth group. Then, through her tears, she shared how she felt about herself, especially her hard-to-manage hair and her bigger-than-average nose. Although I thought she was a bit sensitive about those areas—she was a nice-looking girl—I listened and accepted and affirmed her. I felt as though our relationship had turned a corner.

But a couple of days later, in a circle of Mollie and her friends, I said something like, "Hey, you girls don't think Mollie's nose is big, do you?" I meant well because I was trying to give her a more positive self-concept. But Mollie's jaw dropped, and her eyes said it all: "How could you!"

And she never came to youth group again.
—Name Withheld

Yet that's exactly what we hope our students will do with us. We want them to trust us enough to share what's behind the mask. We want to help them find solutions to their problems, healing for their hurts, and answers to their questions. And nothing can destroy a relationship quicker than a broken confidence. Consider these possibilities:

- As an illustration for a talk, a youth director tells a true story about a girl in the group without first getting her permission.
- In an attempt to convince a senior football player to come to an event, a youth leader tells him about a couple of girls in the group who think he's pretty cool.
- While playing basketball, a student gives the adult leader a hard foul. The leader angrily responds by blurting out private, privileged information about the player.
- During a conversation with a group of kids, the youth ministry volunteer responds to one student's assertion by saying, "But you told me..."
- In a letter to donors, a staff member of a parachurch ministry shares a true story about a young person with enough details that almost anyone can figure out who's being described, even though the name has been changed.
- In an effort to build a friendship with one student, a youth worker shares a secret of another student.

And you probably can imagine some other trust-destroying scenarios. Students need to know that what they tell us in private stays private.

But there are exceptions.

This privacy rule doesn't apply to *everything* you hear—quite the contrary. In fact, most states have laws compelling those who hear stories of abuse or plans for crimes to report that information to the proper authorities.

And what about suicide talk? Think of how you'd feel if a young person confided that she'd been thinking about ending it all, and you did or said nothing...and the person followed through on the threat.

So here are a few guidelines:

- Never promise to keep a secret that you're *required* to share, a confidence that you're required to break.
- Explain to your group and to individuals, when appropriate, that you will *not* keep quiet if someone is being harmed or will be harmed by the information that's been shared (suicide, fights, crimes, abusive situations, and so on).

- Explain that everything else will be held in strictest confidence (such as feelings about self, relationship dramas, worries, fears, dreams, opinions, and conflicts with parents, teachers, or coaches).

Some youth leaders have learned this lesson the hard way. They wish they'd known then what they know now.

Discussion Questions

1. Why do some people find it so difficult to keep secrets?

2. When do you feel the most pressured to share something you've been told in confidence?

3. How do your students know they can trust you?

4. What will you do when you have to break a confidence because of the potential harm?

For Further Study

• In his classic book *Why Am I Afraid to Tell You Who I Am?* John Powell says, "I'm afraid to tell you who I am because you may not like who I am, and that's all I have." Think about the implications of that statement for youth ministry and other relationships.

• Reread these classic passages, considering how they apply to building relationships with students: Proverbs 17:17; 18:24; Matthew 7:12; and Romans 12:10.

• Ask a professional counselor or social worker about the laws relating to confidentiality.

Avoiding an Avoidable Mess

• Meet with your ministry staff. Read the above examples of breaking and losing trust with teenagers and discuss what you all can do to build trust with your students.

• At the same meeting, explain your confidentiality policy and its implications for students, parents, the church, and the youth ministry.

PLAYING FAVORITES

Relational ministry is tricky. Jesus tells us to love *everyone*: Family members, fellow believers, neighbors, employers—even enemies. In fact, at one time or another, you'll probably have to deal with every one of those categories of people in your youth ministry. Okay, maybe none of the students in your group fit neatly into the "enemies" category, but I bet a few of them are pretty obnoxious. Relating to those kids, let alone "loving" them, is hard work.

At the other end of the spectrum, certain students are just fun to be around—they laugh at our jokes, seem to hang on our every word, and hardly ever cause us any grief. And if we're not careful, we'll spend most of our time with those kids and avoid the others. Many young youth ministers make that mistake.

J.T. Bean shares his experience with this issue:

> Just after my fortieth birthday, I retired from youth ministry after 17 years. I think one of the reasons I was able to stay in the game for that long was my ability to connect with kids of all kinds. I was often told that one of my strengths was that I didn't play favorites. I was accepting of students whoever they were and whatever they looked like or acted like.
>
> Honestly, not playing favorites is hard. I've had many kids during my youth ministry career who were difficult to love. Some of them I secretly wished would invite themselves to another group so they could be somebody else's problem. But as I networked with other youth workers, I quickly realized that the grass was not greener—every group has that same kind of kid who requires extra grace.
>
> In fact, I believe God puts these kinds of people in our churches to test us. He tests our patience, the limits of our love, and our ability to set an example for those we lead.

But what about Jesus? Didn't Jesus have favorites? Weren't Peter, James, and John in his inner circle?

Certainly, Jesus seemed to give those three disciples special attention. But rather than being "favorites," perhaps they were the most needy. Remember, James and John were nicknamed "sons of thunder" (Mark 3:17) probably because of their tempers. And impetuous Peter seemed to be focused on himself—he certainly suffered from foot-in-mouth disease.

At times, the effective youth director will have to spend concentrated bites of time with certain individuals for any number of reasons. That's the way life happens. And some students will have more time available than others, so leaders will end up logging more time with them.

Note, too, that connection is not the same thing as favoritism. Expect that you'll naturally be drawn to certain students and not to others—it's a fact of life. You're going to be in sync with some students. You'll have a connection.

And let's be honest: Those students may turn out to be your "favorites." But that doesn't mean you have to demonstrate favoritism. In fact, we need to go out of our way not to favor one kid over another. They get plenty of that with their friends and in the neighborhood.

We dare not fall into class distinctions in youth ministry, with an in-crowd and everyone else on the outside looking in. That's the way the world (school) operates, not the church. We should be known for our love and acceptance. The youth group should be a positive, welcoming, safe community.

Discussion Questions

1. When have you been tempted to play favorites in your ministry? What happened?

2. When you were in high school, were you part of the "in-crowd" or "out-crowd"? How did someone become part of the popular group?

3. When have you seen that played out in church settings? Were you part of the "in-crowd" there? Again, how did someone get in that group?

4. What can you and your staff do to reach out to the shy kids, the kids on the fringes, the apathetic and defiant kids, and the obnoxious ones?

It took me a long time to realize that in a relational ministry setting you'll be drawn to certain kids—and that's all right. For a long time, I felt guilty because I connected with some kids more than others, and I often tried to correct this by trying to force relationships that just weren't happening.
—Rob Hankins

For Further Study
• Meditate on Matthew 25:31-46. Then consider who the "least of these" might be in your youth ministry circle.
• Read James 2:1-13 and consider how the passage relates to your youth group.

Avoiding an Avoidable Mess
• In a staff meeting, preferably at the beginning of the ministry year, design a practical strategy to make sure every student in your group has a staff person who's working to build a relationship with that youth.

• Either during that same meeting or a later one, expand that strategy for reaching out to others who aren't in the youth ministry but should be.

• Make sure your ministry is a safe place where no one is left out or excluded.

COMMUNICATING TRUTH

Ours is a verbal faith.
Eternal realities and divine mysteries…
Spoken.
Written.
Prophets and preachers.
Missionaries bearing messages from heaven.
Apostles composing epistles.
Using God-given verbs and adverbs.
The eternal on parchment.
The written word about the Word made flesh.
Transforming truth.

In a world filled with fallacies and conflicting ideas, students need truth. More than anything else, they need spiritual leaders who will unashamedly and creatively declare God's life-changing Word.

If I knew then what I know now—if I could start all over—I'd make sure my youth ministry was built upon a strong biblical foundation.

BIBLE 101

It's been said that when it comes to a "can't miss" curriculum for your youth group, you will *always* have an audience if you talk about:

a. Sex and Dating, or
b. The End Times

And if you *really* want crowds of students at your meetings, you might consider doing a series on "Will there be *sex and dating* DURING the *end times*?"

I (Len) never tried that third option. For that matter I never attempted to walk through the theological minefield of what the Bible says about the return of Christ. I confess I talked often about love, sex, and dating—

because as a just-out-of-college single guy, I was as interested in those topics as any of my students were. But let's face it: The spiritual life is about much more than just "romantic relationships."

Here's the bottom line truth: When I became a youth pastor, all I had in the way of "preparation" was a strong Southern Baptist upbringing. (Translation: Lots of time logged in Sunday school, Vacation Bible School, youth group, and revival meetings.) I also had some basic Campus Crusade training. But I had no seminary or Bible college degree. In fact, I'm not sure I'd even read the entire Bible yet. Therefore, I didn't know the Bible very well, and I didn't know how to study it for myself.

I could parrot talks that I'd heard others give. (And I'm ashamed to say I sometimes did—often without giving them proper credit.) I also got great help from Youth Specialties' *Ideas Library*. But come up with original messages out of my own disciplined study? Nope. I hadn't yet developed that skill.

Here's what I learned: You don't have to be a seminary grad, much less a Bible scholar, to work effectively with teenagers—but you do need to believe the Bible is God's inspired Word, his authoritative Truth for life. And you need an ever-increasing understanding of what it says.

At some point you have to know something—or at least be willing to learn some things. You can't easily lead teenagers to a place you've never been. To quote the legendary Dr. Howard Hendricks, "You cannot impart that which you do not possess."

Here are some of the other lessons I learned:

- You can give the same messages (or variations of the same messages) only so many times.
- You can wing it for only so long.
- If you stop learning and growing, then your group will soon follow suit.
- Ripping off the talks of youth experts or great conference speakers is neither ethical nor effective. Be yourself—not a bad impersonation of Rob Bell, Andy Stanley, Beth Moore, or Mark Driscoll. Learn from them but be yourself. Remember, God can speak *to* you directly and *through* you powerfully—and he longs to do so!
- In order to have the greatest impact, God's Word needs to enter your mind, mess with your heart and will, and *then* (and only then) come out of your mouth. Skip that second step and you're just giving cerebral book reports on the Bible. And if it's just a book report, your students can probably find better ones online.
- Being in a situation where you *have something to say* is a whole lot better than being in place where you *have to say something*.

Learning to study the Bible for yourself, and then actually developing the discipline to do that (day by day), will help you hear from God on a more regular basis. Then you'll have something fresh and worthwhile to pass on to the students under your care—and do it with passion and authenticity.

Discussion Questions

1. On a scale of 1 to 10 (with 1 being "anemic" and 10 being "amazing"), rate your current Bible knowledge.

2. How can some Christians claim great belief in God and devotion for God but then go for years—or maybe an entire lifetime—without bothering to read what he's revealed?

3. Have *you* ever read through the entire Bible? If not, why?

4. Is it possible to be effective as a youth pastor or director if you don't know the Bible that well? In other words, would it work to just bring in other knowledgeable and gifted folks to do all the teaching?

For Further Study

• Spend some time reflecting on 2 Timothy 3:16-17. What if we *really* believed that passage is true—that every word of Scripture is breathed by God and can help us have the kind of life we've always wanted?

• Meditate on Hebrews 4:12.

Avoiding an Avoidable Mess

• Read the Bible from cover to cover. Granted, it seems massive—all that tiny print on hundreds of onionskin pages. Yet, if you break it down into manageable chunks—three chapters a day and five on Sundays—you can read the entire Bible in a year. Early in my marriage and ministry, I [Len] did this several years in a row. I was amazed at the difference that 15 to 20 minutes a day made. And the habit helped me acquire a much broader knowledge of the Bible.

• Take a basic course in Bible study methods. Look online or get together with a couple of ministry colleagues and work through Dave Veerman's *How to Apply the Bible*.

• Invest in a basic biblical library. Ask your pastor or ministry director to recommend a good atlas, Bible dictionary, Bible encyclopedia, and a one- or two-volume commentary set. Or purchase and learn to use a good Bible software program such as WordSearch (www.WordSearchBible.com). The investment of time and money in learning to use these tools will pay rich dividends.

BEING CREATIVE

A lot has been said and written about the short attention spans of this generation. Many teenagers and young adults seem unable to track with a speaker for more than five minutes. Want to keep your audience? Then you've gotta spice things up—throw in a homemade short film, a crazy YouTube video, a guy juggling Bibles or gerbils, and an object lesson on faith involving someone bungee jumping from the church rafters.

Contrast this state of affairs with stories about how during colonial times, many preachers would *read* their two-hour sermons in a monotone voice, the congregation reportedly riveted to every syllable of every word.

What's up with that? Is our inability to focus the fault of watching too much TV? Does it stem from watching too many movies with lots of quick edits? Music videos? Is the Internet somehow to blame? Maybe the situation has something to do with our diet—treating our bodies like living chemistry sets by shoving all kinds of processed food into our pie holes—sugary junk filled with preservatives and chemical additives. Why the surge in the number of children diagnosed with ADD or ADHD?

I (Len) remember one youth meeting during which we decided to have a volunteer worker suddenly crank up his motorcycle just outside the youth room and race across the front of the assembly. I don't even remember what the point of this was (was there one?). But I promise

IDEAS FOR CREATIVE COMMUNICATION

- Short skits (well rehearsed in advance!)
- Short video clips (always previewed!)
- Brief testimonies or quick interviews that illustrate a point
- Audience participation ("neighbor nudges," "raise your hand," and so on)
- Tag-team teaching
- Great stories
- Effective PowerPoint (but not overused)
- Appropriate humor
- Quick object lessons
- Trinkets—that is, something for each person to take home (For example, a small river rock to carry in one's pocket as a reminder that God is our Rock and Refuge (Psalm 18:2).)

Mark Oestreicher addresses the common misconception among youth workers that the "best curriculum is the stuff I write." He writes, "Okay, I'll admit it. I'm letting my bias as the publisher at Youth Specialties show. But these are statements I hear all the time:

- 'I don't trust curriculum from publishers;

I'd rather write my own.'
- 'I've never found anything on this subject, so I wrote it.' (This usually comes attached to a proposal for a book product that has 50 look-alikes on the market already.)

"Here's the deal: you may be able to write kickin' materials. But it will take you a long time—time that could be spent doing other ministry functions. And occasionally, you may teach a subject that is truly outside any resource available. But the reality is that good writers and publishers have prepared stuff for your use in ministry, and much of it is well done.

"So, a one-word revision to this misconception makes it a wonderfully true statement: The best curriculum is the stuff I *modify*.

"I never teach straight out of a printed resource. Even the best curriculum writer doesn't know my students, my community, my church, me. I have to modify it. I could rant on this one for 50 more pages, but 'nuf said."

you, whatever it was—it got lost in a cloud of motorbike exhaust.

We could say a lot about what makes for effective teaching. But we won't. Instead, we'll settle for two bits of simple counsel: (1) Lose the lecture, and (2) Keep 'em guessing.

Numerous studies have proven that lectures simply aren't effective. Very few speakers can stand in front of a group, deliver a lengthy monologue, and keep the audience's attention.

Having said that, another truth is that one-way communication is improved when more variety is introduced—props, stories, humor, video, drama, pictures, and so forth. This is because people have different learning styles. Some are auditory learners, but more are visual learners. They have to see a truth before it sticks. And then there's the wise old saying: "I hear, I forget. I see, I remember. I do, I understand."

So engaging the audience, getting them to participate, is huge. Creativity and variety can help accomplish this. But remember, if used in a haphazard or amateurish way, innovative elements can actually distract from the overall message. How many times has a youth leader shown a video clip, and the audience remembers the clip but not the point?

Not only should we lose the lecture, but we also need to keep the audience guessing, never letting them know what's coming next. We want to give everyone that sense of, "I don't want to miss group tonight. I'm not exactly sure *what's* going to happen, but I know I'm going to hear something true and powerful, and it's going to be presented in a creative and memorable way."

Discussion Questions

1. What's your *style* as a communicator? Are you a classic orator? A storyteller? A passionate exhorter? A persuader? A conversationalist? A teacher imparting knowledge? What?

2. What strengths do you have when it comes to communicating God's truth? What are your weaknesses?

3. If you could focus on getting better in one specific area of communicating, what would it be?

For Further Study

• Read the Gospels. Note how Jesus communicated to both big groups and small ones. Study the Sermon on the Mount (Matthew chapters 5-7). Reflect on the parables he told.

• Ponder Acts 18:24-28. What made Apollos such an effective communicator?

Avoiding an Avoidable Mess

• Watch or listen to excellent communicators of all kinds—top-rated TV anchors, motivational speakers, big-name conference presenters, popular pastors, and effective politicians. The goal isn't to impersonate them but to analyze why they're effective. What do they do that makes you want to listen? How do they manage to get you to remember what they've said?

• Watch creative comedians (not the ones who get laughs by being vulgar, but the ones who are humorous *and insightful*). Really good comics and humorists are great students of human nature who observe the quirks and eccentricities of life.

• Have someone videotape you as you speak and force yourself to watch it. What do you do that's boring? How do you use your face, body, and voice in creative ways?

KEEPING IT SIMPLE

Most youth workers are able to spend, at most, maybe eight hours a week with their most committed students, tops (unless it happens to be a mission trip week or a retreat weekend). Figure two or three hours on Sunday (unless you're a parachurch youth worker), a couple more at some kind of midweek meeting or Bible study, and maybe another small slice of time at a church or school event.

Each week has only 168 hours, which means we have access to our most committed Christian teenagers for, at most, 5 percent of their time during the few years they're with us.

Annually, we have access to devoted church kids for, oh, let's say 40 to 45 Sundays. And maybe they attend a similar number of youth meetings. That gives us a maximum of 80 to 90 shots at an extremely devoted student's heart and mind each year. Eighty-five chances to speak into his life. Eighty-five opportunities to teach him about God.

Now, let's say we have that highly involved kid for six years (seventh through twelfth grades). Add retreats and camps to the equation; then subtract absences due to illness, schedule conflicts, and family vacations. What you're left with is—at most—about 500 "official" chances to teach and train. And that's for the most committed students whose families don't relocate.

That may sound like a lot of opportunities. But remember, we live in a big, ever-changing, messy, scary world filled with a myriad of mysteries, concerns, and questions. Time flies in the Information Age. New issues arise out of the blue. We can easily become reactive, following every new trend that emerges and becoming haphazard in what we teach.

If I knew then what I know now, I'd have made the proactive, conscious decision to stick to a few basics. I'd have sat down in the first days of my tenure and come up with an irreducible minimum.

What basic biblical truths do I want students to understand upon leaving the group? What essential spiritual disciplines do I want my youth to practice? What character qualities would I like to see growing in them?

I'd sit down with my advisory team and my volunteer workers and list those things—the fundamental beliefs, nonnegotiable behaviors, and essential virtues. And that's where I'd camp. I'd hammer them over and over. I'd come at them from every possible angle. Again and again. Reminding. Restating. Rephrasing. Teaching and reteaching. I'd embrace a simplified curriculum of the basics.

Once I had my list of essentials, I'd get out the calendar and start scheduling exactly how and when we'd go about creatively emphasizing each of them. A planned series here. A scheduled message there. I'd avoid the common "hot topic *du jour*" approach, and I'd be more intentional, more systematic, more disciplined, more focused. I'd opt for the important over the weird, the essentials over the tangents. I'd "preach (and teach) the Word" (2 Timothy 4:2).

We might think, *If we just teach the Bible, our students will be bored. They won't come.* Not true. Rob Bell started the wildly successful Mars Hill Bible Church in Michigan by preaching the entire first year out of Leviticus! Yes, *that* Leviticus!

If I could sit down with you over coffee, first I'd try to twist your arm to pay for my latte. But then I'd encourage you to make the front-end decision, "I'm not going to be the person who talks superficially about 894 things. I'm going to camp out on these three big themes, or I'm going to pound away at these 10 overarching truths. Or our theme verse is going be the Great Commission. That's it."

Experts say the secret to Ronald Reagan's success as a U.S. president was his ability to stay focused on a few things. Now, maybe you don't regard him as successful; perhaps you weren't even alive when he was elected. But most historians, regardless of their political persuasion, agree that Reagan was an effective leader. He accomplished much of what he set out to do— and not just because he happened to be "The Great Communicator." Unlike so many politicians who feel the need to roll out new initiatives daily, most historians agree that Reagan was guided by a couple of big, overriding ideas: Defeating communism by being strong militarily, and reducing the size and power of the federal government. Two big initiatives instead of 222 smaller ones.

When we consider individual talks or messages, the same principle applies. We can dump every idea we have onto the group each week. We can confuse them by trying to make 37 points. (I actually heard a speaker once emphasize—during a single message—"Pray a lot; share your faith; obey your parents; stay sexually pure; be careful what movies you watch; be kind..." and so on. They're a bunch of good

Lots of times we think, *I've got to come up with the perfect message.* But think about your own memories from youth group. What did you take away? Do you really remember all the specifics of all those Bible lessons your youth leader gave? Do you remember the detailed points of his messages? Or do you remember the time spent in relationships? I'd bet that's what sticks with you—the youth leaders and volunteers who invested in you, the relationships you enjoyed.

I think if you can boil down each message to one or two pretty simple (and memorable) statements of truth and then keep hammering them, you'll be more effective. In my former youth group, our mission statement was "Love God and love people." Obviously, there are a million different aspects and angles to that, but the overarching and underlying message over and over was, "How are you loving God better, and how are you loving others more?" Are you loving God by spending time with him? Are you loving people by serving them? And I just kept hammering away at that, understanding that if I tried to impart every minute facet of theological truth to my students, then not only would they walk away with this vague, blurry sense of the faith, but I'd also feel constantly frustrated, and nobody would be helped.

—John O'Leary

and true thoughts, but it's a blurry flurry of information.) Or we can keep it simple. One big idea communicated each time you gather. One memorable point. Tell it. Prove it. Demonstrate it. Show it. Illustrate it. Apply it. Underline it. Emphasize it. Then a few weeks later or maybe next month, bring it up again.

Discussion Questions

1. This question deserves concentrated thought over an extended period of time: What are the essentials you want your students to "have" when they graduate from your group?

2. How does intentional planning help simplify life and ministry?

3. What's the difference between being simple and being overly simplistic?

For Further Study

• Reflect on Luke 15. Jesus tells three short stories. What is the central idea of his teaching in these parables?

• Read Paul's counsel to a young minister in 2 Timothy 2:15. What does Paul urge regarding Timothy's ability to handle the Word?

Avoiding an Avoidable Mess

• Read the book *Made to Stick: Why Some Ideas Survive and Others Die* by Chip and Dan Heath (Random House, 2007). This provocative secular work asks why few messages are memorable, and most are quickly forgotten.

BEING A TEAM PLAYER

Clint was a great guy, a very committed follower of Christ, and a volunteer Bible study leader with our student ministry. God was using him. Things were going well. But he came from a church background with some different theological views than ours. And before long, he began to express those beliefs and encouraged others to embrace them as well.

His actions and teachings confused a lot of students. So I (Len) had to address his actions. I did so gently but firmly. Still, the confrontation didn't go well. He ended up leaving the church and our student group in a huff. And a few others went with him.

Because you're reading this book, the chances are good that you're working with a preexisting organization (that is, you're *not* the founder, president, and CEO of your own youth ministry or church). This means you've joined a group with a history. You've linked up with an entity with a definitive doctrinal statement, an established philosophy of ministry, and a clearly stated mission.

This further means that the folks who hired you almost surely didn't bring you there in order for you to set them straight. For the most part, they probably like what they're doing and the direction in which they're headed. They want your contributions. But they don't need or want you to be upsetting the apple cart.

Here's a good rule of thumb: If you can't in good conscience and with wholehearted enthusiasm support and further your church's mission and the ministry's goals, then you need to have the integrity to go elsewhere.

Bottom line: Be a team player...or get off the team.

Discussion Questions

1. What's the difference between conformity and unity?

2. When is the appropriate time for individuals to question an organization's

DON'T FORGET:

- Teenagers get bombarded with hundreds of messages daily (by companies that spend millions of bucks on slick advertising created by experts in human nature). What makes you think your 12-point message is going to penetrate and stick?
- Keep the main things the main things.
- If you can't summarize the main idea of your message, then be assured that when you're finished, your audience won't be able to either. As the old saying goes, "If it's a mist in the pulpit, it's a fog in the pew!"
- More is actually less. And less is ironically more!
- According to the legendary preaching professor, Haddon Robinson, the Bible contains only a dozen or so "big ideas." That's why the Scriptures have so much repetition.
- Folks have to hear something repeatedly before they'll remember it.

I was in a ministry situation once where my directional leader shared her vision—and I didn't exactly regard it as the most compelling vision I'd ever heard. Actually, I thought it was pretty lame and that her proposed direction left a lot to be desired. So what did I do? Muster up the integrity to leave? No. Did I buy in anyway and support the organization's mission with all my heart and soul? Not so much. I rolled my eyes a lot. I grumbled, made snide comments about the state of affairs, and, in the process, poisoned a younger colleague.

In hindsight I was, if you can say this in a Christian book for Christian ministers, a butthead. Shame on me. May God forgive my passive rebellion.

—Anonymous

purpose or direction? What about pushing to *change* an existing organization's goals or mission?

3. The renowned theologian Augustine once said: "In essentials, unity; in nonessentials, liberty; in all things, charity." How might this statement apply to the topic under discussion?

4. What are the qualities that make for a great, smooth-running team? How about for a quality team player?

For Further Study
• Spend some time reflecting on 2 Samuel 15:1-6. What did Absalom, son of David, do to create leadership problems for his father—and ultimately for the nation of Israel?

• Meditate on Philippians 2:1-11.

Avoiding an Avoidable Mess
• Make sure you have a copy of your ministry's doctrinal statement. Get familiar with it. If you have questions about any of the doctrines, discuss them with your supervisor. Commit to advocate those beliefs and not your own unique theological ideas.

• Make sure you understand and can articulate your church or organization's ministry philosophy. More importantly, make sure you're onboard with it.

• If you have questions about an idea for a new venture, ministry project, or teaching initiative and whether or not it fits within the parameters of your organization, then stop everything and discuss the matter with your supervisor, staff director, or advisory team.

DEALING WITH **PARENTS**

I (Dave) walked into the school as I'd done hundreds of time as a Campus Life staff member. Turning right, I pushed open the doors to the administrative offices and introduced myself to the secretary—"I'm Dave Veerman, Kara's father." Then I asked if I could see the principal. Surprisingly, after making a quick call, she ushered me into the principal's office where he greeted me warmly. Then, even more of a surprise, after I explained about Campus Life/JV and my desire to sponsor a club for the school and use the multipurpose room or gym from time to time, the principal smiled and said he was sure that wouldn't be a problem.

Over the next few weeks and months I discovered that simply being a parent of a student in the school offered me opportunities and privileges that had been quite difficult to obtain in my professional role. Issues I often faced when I'd entered the school as a "youth minister"— such as concerns about the separation of church and state, having to "obtain school board approval," and so forth—were gone. Instead of being viewed as an outsider who probably wanted to use the school for *my* purposes (religious, commercial, or whatever), I was seen as an insider and an ally.

I also found myself doing naturally, as a parent, what I'd been paid to do as a youth worker—spending time with kids by driving them places (Kara and her friends always needed rides); walking freely through the school to visit teachers, coaches, and administrators; attending games, plays, and concerts; and sponsoring school events.

My new role as a parent of a teenager opened my eyes to certain truths about working with kids and gave me greater empathy for the challenges parents face. And each time, I thought, *I wish I'd known then what I know now about being a parent.*

MAKING ALLIES (NOT ENEMIES)

A common mistake of newly minted youth workers is viewing parents as adversaries. This happens for any number of reasons:

- A mom complains that the youth group is much too serious and bores her teenager.
- A dad complains that the youth group provides only fun and games and not enough "meat."
- A teenage girl complains how her parents are so out of touch.
- A number of students give examples of their parents' issues and mistakes during a youth group discussion.

Parents mess up their kids for 15 years and then expect us to fix them in a couple of hours a week.
—*Anonymous Youth Worker*

After just one of these incidents, the youth worker, without realizing it, may begin to avoid parents. Or he may simply hunker down in the ministry and ignore the parents altogether. In both cases, the silence and distance between the youth leader and the parents grows.

Despite the occasional (and painful) exceptions, most parents are on our side—they really are. They want the youth ministry to be successful. They want us to be successful. Because they want the best for their children and want them to be safe, they will ask tough questions about ministry approaches and activities. They'll be concerned about what goes on in all the youth activities and events. Instead of feeling threatened and seeing those questions as unwelcome intrusions in our territory, we should see them as positive signs that parents care.

Parents come in all shades and types, so we're likely to encounter a few with chips on their shoulders or hidden agendas. But most parents want to be supportive—really. So we should see them as allies, not enemies.

Parents love their kids. And most of them would love to work *with* those who lead and guide their children: Teachers, coaches, music directors, and, yes, even youth ministers.

Parents can give us invaluable insights into what their kids are like and what they're going through. They know their offspring better than anyone else—their temperaments, talents and gifts, strengths and weaknesses, and dreams and desires. And most parents understand the need to receive support, encouragement, and guidance—for their teens and for themselves—from people like us.

If I knew then what I know now, I would have spent more time getting to know the parents, communicating with them about my goals for the ministry and their kids, and partnering with them.

Discussion Questions

1. What evidence do you have that the parents of the students in your group care about their kids?

2. What evidence do those parents have that *you* care about their kids?

3. In what ways could you help parents be more effective in parenting their teenagers?

4. How might the parents help you in the ministry?

5. How might you be able to help parents in *their* ministry with their kids?

For Further Study

• Read Deuteronomy 6:6-7; Psalm 113:9; 127:3-5; Proverbs 13:24; 22:6; Matthew 18:1-6; Ephesians 6:4; and 1 John 4:7-12 and ask how each passage applies to the parents of the students in your group. Also consider how they apply to you in youth ministry.

• Read chapter 4, "Parents: Friends or Foes?" from *Dave's Complete Guide to Junior High Ministry* by Dave Veerman (available electronically through WordSearch).

Avoiding an Avoidable Mess

• Pull together a parents' advisory council for your youth ministry. Such a group can provide invaluable counsel and help you communicate with other parents.

• Communicate regularly with all parents of the kids in your group, through emails, personal notes and letters, newsletters, phone calls, and face to face.

• Sponsor a special seminar for parents, such as those offered by Home-Word (www.HomeWord.com/seminars/)—for example, "Understanding Your Teenager" and "Generation 2 Generation."

KEEPING PARENTS IN THE LOOP

One Sunday morning, I (Len) led our ninth graders in a discussion of priorities. I especially wanted them to ponder their lives in light of Christ's Great Commandment (Matthew 22:37-40). I wanted them to remember that two things matter above all else—God and people.

To get them thinking, I had my group do a modified version of an exercise I'd seen in one of Youth Specialties' *Ideas* books. As I recall, my adaptation went something like this:

> A foreign government has decided that you guys are too good-looking and too smart. You have too much talent and faith, and you possess a dangerous level of leadership ability. Bottom line: You represent a serious threat to their evil plans. In fact, because of your awesome potential to change the world, this government has just launched a military strike. From a submarine just off the coast, they've fired a cruise missile at this one classroom.
>
> The bad news is that in exactly 15 minutes we will all be vaporized. However, the good news is that I have some special bombproof writing paper that can withstand any such attack. So here's the plan: We're going to use the next few minutes to write short notes to the person who means the most to us. We don't have time to discuss superficial matters like the weather. This is your time to say what is most on your heart. Begin writing *now*. Don't goof off! The clock is ticking.[2]

With that somber instruction, the group began writing feverishly. The room was deadly quiet. My exercise was a huge hit (no pun intended). Following the imaginary blast, we had a lively discussion about priorities, about why we fritter our lives away on superficial stuff. We ended with a challenge to live every day like it might be our last, to focus on people and not things.

One summer afternoon a few months later, I came home to find several urgent phone messages for me to call Jennifer's mom. (This was in the days before cell phones and pagers.) My roommate added that everyone—the pastor, assorted youth parents, and the associate pastor—had all been frantic to find me.

I picked up the phone and dialed Jennifer's home. No answer. So I called one of my colleagues, and this is what he said: "Len, we've got a

2. It never occurred to me at the time—and obviously it didn't occur to any of my students either—but there was a gaping plot hole in my hypothetical scenario. If we knew a missile was on the way and we had 15 minutes to do something, why not just leave the building and drive as fast and as far away as we could? Or we could at least wrap ourselves in the bombproof writing paper.

crisis on our hands. Jennifer left last night on a flight to go visit a friend in Texas. And this morning, her mother found what appears to be a suicide note on Jennifer's desk."

"What?!" I blurted. "Jennifer? Impossible! I can't see that in a million years. What does the note say?"

"Well, it's pretty grim…something along the lines of 'Mom, I guess I'll never see you again. I'll be in heaven soon. But I want you to know a few things. I'm sorry for all the times I've treated you bad. I do love you so much. Thank you for everything you've done for me. I wish we could have many more years together, but there's no way out. Please don't be sad. I'm okay. Take care. I love you. Jennifer.'"

I felt sick to my stomach. I couldn't believe it. I knew the death of Jennifer's dad last year had been a terrible blow. But I thought she was grieving healthily. I would have sworn she was solid. "So have they found her?" I asked. "What about her friend—have they talked?"

"Well, when her mom couldn't get a hold of you or anyone at the friend's home in Texas, she hopped a flight to Dallas. She's hopeful she can get there in time."

Several moments of silence passed while I racked my brain trying to make sense of everything. Suddenly, a thought flashed through my head. "Wait a minute!" I blurted. "I wonder if that 'suicide note' is a Sunday school exercise we did a few months back."

"You had the kids write *suicide notes*?"

"No!" I replied. Then I briefly explained the lesson. The longer we talked, the more my hunch made sense. Sure enough, within a few hours a very shocked daughter and a very relieved mother were embracing—400 miles from home! A giant misunderstanding. A costly mess. But a happy ending.

The moral of the story (and the stern instructions from my bosses)? Make sure that all future creative learning exercises are labeled or titled YOUTH GROUP LESSON!

Discussion Questions

1. What's the most creative youth lesson you've ever dreamed up or participated in?

2. Why is it important to ally yourself with the parents of your students? To seek to build relationships with them and partner with them?

For Further Study
• Reflect on the statement in 1 Peter 2:17—"Show proper respect to everyone." How might this apply (practically and specifically) to a youth worker's dealings with parents?

• Ponder 1 Peter 5:5 and its implications for working with parents.

• Spend some time meditating on 1 Timothy 4:11-16.

Avoiding an Avoidable Mess
• Schools routinely offer open houses where faculty members give parents an overview of what topics the students will be covering in each subject area during the semester. Shouldn't youth groups do the same thing? Such communication lessens the possibility of misunderstanding. It also acts as a healthy kind of accountability. By publicizing your plans, you tie your hands—in a good sense.

• When planning to discuss potentially controversial topics like sex (or drugs and rock 'n' roll), make sure you give parents a heads-up. If you're using a video curriculum, you could even provide a chance for interested parents to preview the material.

PARTNERING WITH PARENTS
In my (Dave) ministry with Campus Life (during my college years and afterward), most of the time I spent with high school students was at their school and extracurricular events, one-on-one, and in our club meetings. I had limited contact with their parents at some of those events, in church, and in students' homes when I picked them up or had a meeting there—but that was about it. Then after a year or two, I began holding "parent meetings," which were more informational in nature.

During those early ministry years, all my staff volunteers were college students or young adults in the community. Certainly I knew parents were important—since all my students came from homes of one type or another—but I didn't see parents as a ministry resource at all, except to host meetings, provide refreshments, donate funds, and, occasionally, provide transportation.

About 20 years later, after I'd begun the "parent of a teenager" life phase, I found the roles reversed. In my role as a parent and not the ministry professional, I was eager to help the youth ministry wherever I could. At about the same time, my wife and I began a junior high ministry at our church. And, as national Campus Life director, I was helping design and test the Campus Life/JV ministry model, which—not so coincidentally—centered on parent volunteers. A few years later—with a daughter now a middle-adolescent—I worked closely with the local Young Life staff, helping them establish a ministry at our high school.

Over the years my philosophy of ministry changed. This was probably because I found that I needed more help—and parents were able and willing—but it was also because, as a parent, I saw the ministry from the other side. As a result, throughout my dozen or so years spent running the junior high ministry at our church (as a layperson), I continually recruited parents as the core volunteers of my ministry team.

We've already discussed that parents know their kids better than anyone and that they want the very best for them. Parents also have insight into adolescent attitudes and actions and family dynamics. And while these parents will need us and other adults to work with their teenagers, they can be a great help with other parents' offspring.

Parachurch ministry differs greatly from church ministry, especially when the emphasis is evangelism and the mission field is the campus. And junior highers are much more open to Mom and Dad attending their events and activities than high schoolers are. Older adolescents like more separation from their parents. But we shouldn't use those realities as excuses for not involving the parents.

If I knew then what I know now, I would have enlisted parents as ministry partners...

- On advisory councils or committees
- As small group leaders
- As teachers
- As counselors of other parents
- As chaperones and emcees
- As friends of students

Discussion Questions

1. What's kept you from utilizing parents in your ministry?

2. To which parents of the teenagers in your group do you feel the most connected?

3. Where do you need help in your ministry to junior high students? To high school students? In what ways could parents meet those needs?

For Further Study
• Read Romans 12:3-5, 1 Corinthians 12:12-31, and Ephesians 4:11-16. Consider your own spiritual gifts and how they might be supplemented by others' gifts.

• Studies continue to show that parents exert the most influence on their children—followed by extended family and other adults (more than peers and media). Consider the implication of this for your ministry.

Avoiding an Avoidable Mess
• The Bible is very clear about parental responsibility for the spiritual development of their children, so discuss with your staff how you can support parents in this process, rather than competing with or hindering them.

• Send a questionnaire to the Christian parents of the students in your group, asking how they'd like to be involved. Be sure to include a list of options.

HOVERING PARENTS
Google *helicopter parents* and you'll find a ton of references in blogs, articles, and editorials. The term refers to parents who "hover" over their children—guiding, protecting, and rescuing them even into late adolescence. These moms and dads can't seem to let go and allow their sons and daughters to become self-reliant adults who make their own way in the world and experience the consequences of their choices and actions, both good and bad.

At birth and for the next few years, parents hover—and they should. Babies and toddlers need almost constant attention and care. But as children grow into later childhood and adolescence, the parents must slowly recede a bit,

I am my child's best advocate.

I know him better than anyone else.

I love him more than any other human ever could.

I have a higher stake in his future than anyone else does.

I am the expert on my child. I know him inside and out, for better and for worse.

I take responsibility for his health, education, and welfare.

And I will make my stand here and now on his behalf.[3]

3. Vicki Caruana, *Standing Up for Your Child Without Stepping on Toes* (Carol Stream, Ill.: Tyndale, 2007), 155.

allowing their children to act more and more on their own. Eventually, at age 18 or so, sons and daughters make a significant break from home and parental control as they go off to college, the military, or careers. The process of letting go can be difficult and painful for parents, some much more than others.

Parents *should* be concerned and involved in their children's lives. What kind of mother or father would allow a son or daughter to be abused, cheated, or led astray? Even in late adolescence, occasions arise that almost demand parental intervention. And certainly all along the way, parents can stay involved to varying extents.

The tension for parents lies in deciding how much to get involved and when and how to back away. At one extreme we have those parents who don't seem to give a rip about their adolescent children, and others who say they care but are absent emotionally, if not physically, from their kids' lives. At the other extreme, we have parents who treat their nearly adult offspring as though they're still in elementary school. But most live somewhere in between, in the tension—they want to be involved but not too much.

We youth workers stand in the middle of parents and their teenagers at this important time in their lives. We have the privilege of interpreting teenagers to their parents and vice versa. And we have a unique opportunity to help teens mature and to help parents let go.

In the grand parenting scheme, hovering parents aren't nearly as problematic as those who are absent. We can applaud these overly concerned moms and dads for their obvious love for their children, and then we can counsel them on the best way to move both them and their adolescents into the next stage of life.

If I knew then what I know now, I'd understand what parents are going through as they release their beloved children to the world—I'd be much more empathetic, and I'd work at helping them make a smooth transition.

Discussion Questions

1. Approximately what percentage of your students has absent or "uncaring" parents? What percentage has overly concerned, "hovering" parents?

2. What evidence do you have of parental hovering?

3. What can you do to celebrate and encourage responsible parental involvement with their kids? In the ministry?

4. How can you help parents who seem to be too involved to slowly back away let go?

For Further Study
• Read *For Parents Only: Getting Inside the Head of Your Kid* by Shaunti Feldhahn and Lisa A. Rice (Multnomah, 2007), especially chapter 2: "Rebel with a Cause."

• Read *The Primal Teen: What the New Discoveries About the Teenage Brain Tell Us About Our Kids* by Barbara Strauch (Doubleday, 2003), especially chapter 14, "Coming of Age."

Avoiding an Avoidable Mess
• Get copies of Dave Veerman's *Letting Them Go: Prepare Your Heart, Prepare Your Child for Leaving Home* (Thomas Nelson, 2006) for the parents of your seniors (or at least make the books available to them).

• At the beginning of the year, when you share ministry goals, programs, and so on with the parents, let them know that you understand the tension of loving their kids and letting them go.

• Make available some copies of *There's a Teenager in My House: 101 Questions Parents Ask* by Wayne Rice, ed. (InterVarsity, 2008) for all your parents.

CRITICAL PARENTS
As I (Dave) walked out of church one sunny Sunday, a parent of one of my students pulled me aside. "Troy told me about your joke about 'necking,' and I don't think that's appropriate," he said with an accusatory tone and a furrowed brow. I told him I didn't remember saying anything like that, assured him I wouldn't allow sexual innuendos, yada yada yada, and we parted ways. On the way home, I replayed that brief conversation in my mind and began to get angry. *How picky—how trivial!* I thought. *Doesn't he know kids are dealing with issues that are way more serious than some offhanded joke or comment that I may or may not have made?* And I fumed.

I was young and somewhat naïve. I hadn't learned that critical parents come with the territory. If I'd known then what I know now, I would have been better prepared to handle those negative or questioning comments.

The truth is we'll always have a few parents who will tend to find fault with just about every aspect of the ministry—they just can't be pleased. Some may have a hidden agenda or peculiar sensitivity (theological, political, or otherwise). Others may be critical because they have unrealistic expectations for us and the church; that is, they fully expect us to *fix* their sons or daughters. And still others may be pessimistic and negative about pretty much everything. But we feel blindsided when these parents suddenly pull us aside, write letters to our superiors, or take us to task publicly.

Fortunately, parents who nitpick and pile on the critical comments are usually the exception, not the rule. And most of the criticisms that parents offer come from a genuine concern for their kids:

- Marge wants her daughter, Tracy, to find a group where she's accepted. (Tracy has few friends at school.)
- Brian is concerned about the direction his son, Kyle, is taking and would love to have a concerned adult come alongside Kyle as a friend and mentor.
- For Susan, the issue is safety. She knows that sometimes the group activities get out of hand.
- Blake's dad keeps pushing for the group to go deeper, helping kids own their faith and pass it on to others.

All these issues are heartfelt and valid. And we need to recognize the parents' feelings and motives and affirm them, even if we can't do everything that each parent asks us to do.

It's a fact of life that people appreciate being included in decisions that affect them. Whether it's done consciously or not, many people take the attitude of *If I'm not in on it, then I'm against it.* When people aren't included in the decision-making process—or even worse, when they're not even informed about a new policy at work, in church, or in the community—they may react negatively and begin to answer their own questions without getting the facts. (Q: Why did they do that? A: I know—it's because...) Then one thing leads to another until the person builds up some serious frustration or anger.

We can stop this downward spiral by practicing more effective communication—getting parents' input early and often and letting them know what we'll be doing and why, all along the way.

Rather than becoming defensive and assuming the worst about parents who criticize us or some aspect of the program, we should understand the motives behind the words and seek to include parents as ministry partners. And we need to be open to their criticisms, too. Believe it or not, parents often have valid and practical insights and ideas for improving the ministry. And if we listen and accept their suggestions, corrections, and admonishments, they'll be more likely to listen to us and to accept ours.

Discussion Questions
1. What criticisms of your ministry have you heard from parents lately? What motivated the critical comments? Which of those criticisms do you believe were valid?
2. What can you do to involve parents in ministry planning?

For Further Study
• Read chapter 6, "Teens Are Developing Personal Values and Beliefs," and Appendix D, "Help from God's Word," from *Understanding Your Teenager* by Wayne Rice and Dave Veerman (Word, 1999).

• Read *Parenting Teens with Love and Logic* (updated and expanded version) by Foster Cline and Jim Fay (NavPress, 2006) and make copies available to parents.

Avoiding an Avoidable Mess
• Either on your own or with all your staff members, brainstorm a list of legitimate concerns that parents of teenagers might have. Include items in these categories: Physical, social, mental, emotional, and spiritual. Then discuss how the ministry can meet those needs and allay those fears.

• Work out a plan with your staff for meeting one-on-one (or in couples) with as many parents as possible, during a two-month period at the beginning of the year.

One parent kept after me about starting an in-depth study of Scripture for those students (actually, his daughter) who didn't feel that our regular weekly lessons were going deep enough. So I did—a study of Mark. Surprisingly, many of my high school students, and a few college students, started to attend the new class on Sunday mornings. And they enjoyed it and thrived in that atmosphere. What I'd initially reacted to defensively turned out to be a good idea.
—*Nate Conrad*

UNCHURCHED PARENTS

Lots of youth groups go horseback riding. But it takes a special group to *kill* a horse. I (Len) once led a group that did that. We rode a horse to death one Saturday.

You've probably been to a dude ranch or camp where they offer the proverbial "trail ride." Everybody gets a helmet and signs a medical waiver. This is followed by riding tips and lots of safety instructions. Then the group heads off slowly, single file, down a meandering well-worn path.

The horses plod. Actually, trudge is more like it. They're clearly bored out of their peanut-sized equine minds. They could do this drill in their sleep, and some apparently do. And then somewhere during the course of the ride, usually when the horses make the big swing back toward the barn, they come alive. They feel especially frisky for a few seconds, and they instinctively begin to trot or canter, achieving speeds of perhaps five miles an hour. That is, until the lead horse suddenly stops, causing a four- or five-horse pile up. Then it's back to a snail's pace—shuffling, pooping, stopping to nibble the grass.

The riding establishment we visited on this particular summer day was different. There were a couple hundred acres of fenced-in wooded property. And there were no organized processions. In fact, there were no rules to speak of. Never rode a horse before? No big deal. It didn't matter. The folks at Runamuck Ranch appeared to follow the "Don't ask. Don't tell" policy. If we signed any forms, I sure don't remember it. Once you got your horse, you were on your own. Giddyap!

Do you remember in the old Western movies when the Apaches or the Sioux would attack a wagon train? Remember how those fearless Native Americans would slip down the side of their horses, somehow hanging on with their legs and firing arrows at the circled settlers, and all while galloping at full speed? Well, all morning we had kids doing a version of that—minus the "arrows," "fearless," and "hanging on" parts. Minus any intentionality, whatsoever. They were just dangling, bouncing, screaming, and occasionally going airborne. Terrified teenagers—on nags with lots of anger issues. I watched one girl get knocked backward off her horse when she failed to duck while passing, against her will, under a thick tree branch.

I may have been born at night, but it wasn't the night before this outing. I quickly realized these horses had sized up our group the moment we stepped off the bus. That would explain the chorus of neighs, whinnies, and stamping feet as we approached the corral and stable. It was all horse code. They had a plan. This was Payback Day. Our group would pay for the sins of all previous youth groups.

I'm not exactly Roy Rogers, but I did my best to ride to the rescue of assorted bruised and terrified kids. About two hours into this ordeal, some worried guys came charging up, yelling, "Come quick! Jeff's horse passed out!"

"What?"

"Yeah, it just keeled over!"

We galloped to the scene and sure enough, Jeff's sweaty steed was lying by a pond, apparently hyperventilating. A few girls looked on tearfully. Guys began speculating on when the buzzards might appear. I exchanged anxious looks with a couple of my college-aged volunteers.

Jeff's parents weren't part of our church—or any church. In fact, they were extremely antagonistic to the ideas of God and church and would often punish Jeff by forbidding him to attend youth activities. Because of their frosty, surly demeanor, I'd always given them a wide berth. I had no relationship with them at all. My only thought was, *When they find out about this, they will never let Jeff come back.*

We did our best with the situation. We tried to comfort the kids (especially Jeff, who was pretty freaked out), and then we sent them all away. I rode back to the office and broke the bad news to the owner of the ranch—who ranted viciously at me for letting Jeff allow his horse to drink too much water. I apologized profusely.

Then I returned to the scene and my helper, and we prayed like we'd never prayed before. I'm not making this up. We literally laid hands on the dying animal before us and asked God to raise it up. To perform an equine miracle. To graciously give this creature a few more years before its appointment at the glue factory.

The poor horse died early the next morning. Just before church, I got a phone call from an irate woman demanding $400 for her dead horse. We paid the bill, and as I'd feared, we didn't see Jeff at youth group for a long time.

I was the pastor of a small church in rural Wisconsin with a staff of one—me. And one of my many responsibilities was the youth program. I recall one unchurched mom and dad whom I got to know primarily through their two daughters who'd grown up in our youth programs. When those girls reached high school, they took home information about a scheduled mission trip to Mexico. The parents were a little concerned about the dangers of travel outside the States, and they asked to talk to me. I was able to reassure them by explaining that I'd lived most of my early years in another country (and look how normal I turned out!), I'd done this trip before, and I could describe the logistics and organizations we'd be utilizing while in Mexico.

One Sunday the girls approached me and asked if there was any chance their parents could go on the trip as chaperones. Frankly, this was a new thought to me. I'd occasionally invited key church members to consider traveling with us (with mixed responses), but I hadn't considered that nonbelieving parents might benefit from a hands-on experience as much as their children. I knew the gospel often becomes especially compelling in a cross-cultural setting (as it often does at camps and on special trips), but I hadn't thought of applying that evangelistic strategy to the folks who often paid the freight for these trips. Ultimately, this couple not only joined that trip, but they eventually traveled with me to several other countries as well—sometimes without kids!

On that first trip to Mexico, they saw and heard the gospel a number of times as it was verbalized by various people on the front lines who were carrying out acts of mercy and justice in Christ's name. And then during our journey home, we stopped on the border in El Paso, Texas, and spent a day debriefing.

We were walking along a sidewalk that parallels the Rio Grande, and we could see Juarez, Mexico, in the distance. Our group was spread out, and I realized this father was walking next to me. He wasn't much of a conversationalist,

What's the lesson here? Can I even boil it down to one? If I knew then what I know now—if I could have a do-over—I'd like to think I would have attempted to cultivate a relationship with Jeff's folks from the beginning, instead of sheepishly avoiding them.

That's pretty basic, right? That's what we're called to do, isn't it? Move toward people with the love of Christ. It's amazing how we can lose sight of the most important things.

If you've got kids whose parents aren't Christians, thank God for those ministry opportunities and proactively seize them. Reach out to the parents every chance you get. Don't wait until bad things happen to get to know them. By then the window of opportunity may be closed.

It's also important to remember that unchurched parents are as concerned about the well-being of their children as any others. They want to know the ins and outs of the ministry, even if they don't ask. Just because they didn't come to the parents meeting at the beginning of the year and haven't invited you into their homes, that doesn't mean they're uninvolved or uncaring. In fact, because their connection to the church or ministry is more distant, maintaining good communication with them is even more important. We want these parents to be for us, not against us.

Unchurched parents may be more suspicious because they don't know us well and, possibly, because they wonder why their adolescent could possibly enjoy something so much, especially when they aren't particularly drawn to anything Christian.

I (Dave) remember leading a trip for high school seniors to a resort in Jamaica. It was just a few months after the Jim Jones (Peoples Temple) tragedy in Guyana. One dad, who didn't know much about Campus Life, wondered aloud to his daughter, and later to me, if we were a cult. Eventually he gave his permission for her to go on the trip. But as she left with us for the airport, his last word of advice (and he was dead serious) was, "Don't drink any Kool-Aid."

Every time you have an opportunity to interact with a parent, take it. Connect with them at events and activities, at their homes when you stop by to see their teenagers, in the parking lot when they drop off or pick up their kids, and out in the community. Better yet, work with your staff at contacting parents in every home the ministry touches, giving information, answering questions, and building relationships.

Another way to build bridges with unbelieving parents is by helping them in their job as parents. Parents of teenagers, especially those whose kids are just entering adolescence, feel vulnerable and insecure. Many are fearful about the teenage years because of what they've read and heard or observed in other homes. Others are concerned by the subtle changes they've seen in their late-elementary school children. Perhaps at no other time in their parenting experience are they so open to outside help and intervention. What a great opportunity to come alongside them as a friend, counselor, and even "youth expert" and in the process share the gospel.

Unbelieving parents, just like all the other parents of teenagers in the world, need help in understanding their kids and in relating to them—and they also need Jesus.

but he suddenly said, "Neil, I need to tell you something. I heard what that speaker said about Romans 10, about confessing your faith with your mouth, and I realized I'd never done that with anyone my whole life. So I decided I would start with you. This trip I definitely crossed the river from being someone who ran my own life to being someone who wants Jesus to run my life from now on." Now, I'd call that a good confession any time!
—Neil Wilson

Discussion Questions

1. Which of your students come from non-Christian homes? What do their parents think of you and the youth ministry?

2. What can you do to assure those parents of your positive motives and goals for their kids?

3. What can you do to involve nonbelieving parents in the ministry?

4. What is your strategy for sharing God's Good News with them?

For Further Study
• Reflect on 1 Peter 3:15-16 and how this principle relates to unbelieving parents or students in your group.

• Meditate on 1 Timothy 4:12, considering what older people are learning about God by watching you.

Avoiding an Avoidable Mess
• Work at communicating ministry purposes, philosophy, and plans to all parents, not just those who attend your church.

• With your staff, design a strategy for ministering to unchurched parents, including praying regularly for them.

COMMON PROGRAMMING MISTAKES

The Law of Entropy states that things tend toward disorder.
For example:

- Paint peels
- Hairlines recede
- Waistlines expand
- Concrete cracks
- Gardens grow weeds
- Engines wear out
- Spotless houses become dusty and messy

Everybody knows that keeping anything from deteriorating takes concerted and consistent effort—and that includes your youth group. If you get distracted or sloppy, then your ministry will quickly become shabby or off-kilter.

One area where this is especially true is in the area of *programming*. You wake up one day and realize your group is focused almost exclusively inward. Why? It's probably because you didn't proactively plan activities to keep them looking outward. Or you notice your group is attracting only the shy, quieter kids. How come? Maybe you've forgotten to schedule some fun, not-so-serious events?

If I knew then what I know now, I'd have been on the lookout for the following programming mistakes...

TOO MUCH "BIG GROUP" AND NOT ENOUGH "SMALL GROUP"

We can easily fall into the trap of believing that if a group of 25 kids is "good," then a group of 50 students must be twice as good. Big groups are great—all that energy, all those teenagers wedged into a slightly too-small meeting space. Add some good music and a good talk that keeps 'em laughing, and everything just clicks. Oh, yeah, baby. That's as good as it gets.

Or so I (Len) once thought.

I don't think that way anymore. In fact, I believe one really good small group discussion in which six or eight kids open up in a safe and supportive environment, talk honestly about their lives, and wrestle with how God's truth applies to their situations is worth a whole series of messages by Buck Studly or Rip Radley or some other dynamic youth speaker.

Big groups are deceptive. The speaker might be good. Maybe she's *really* good. And the crowd might appear to be into it. Laughing. Nodding. Learning? Processing? Maybe. But how do you know for sure? Nobody interrupts to ask a clarifying question. Nobody blurts out, "Hey, say that again!" Individuals *seem* to be tracking right along. You *assume* they're getting it. But are they? Is the speaker—regardless of how dynamic she is—addressing the real struggles of *this* audience at *this* time? That's the dilemma of big groups and large meetings. In a group of 50 or 100 or 250, you can't possibly check in with each person.

Which is why good small groups are so amazing. They're dialogues, not one-way lectures. Maybe just 5 or 10 people. Not strangers, but friends. Discussing. Debating. Back and forth. Intensely. Inquisitively? Small groups offer feedback. And there's this: If the group members are authentic when they speak out and intense when they listen—not just to the words, but to the deeper message of the heart—then the impact on souls is deep, and the potential for life change is huge.

In a big group, all the chairs face forward, and people mostly see the backs of other people's heads. But in a small group, we turn and face each other. We make eye contact. And sometimes our hearts connect, too.

In a big group, we can deliver scattershot information to the audience. In a small group, we can shepherd one another.

I'm not saying big meetings have no place. But I *am* saying be careful to create some more intimate forums where students can take off their masks and be real. Don't undervalue the *big* things God can do in small groups.

Discussion Questions

1. What's been your own small group experience?

2. Do you naturally gravitate toward larger group events or ministry that's structured around smaller groups?

3. List the benefits of big groups. Then list the benefits of small groups.

4. List the negatives of big groups. Then list the negatives of small groups.

5. What's necessary for a youth group to utilize small groups effectively?

For Further Study

• Spend some time reflecting on Matthew 4:18-22. Jesus called a few disciples to be part of his "small group." He spent some time with the masses, but he spent much more time with his "small group." He poured into them.

• Meditate on Acts 2:42-47. This passage illustrates both the big-group aspect ("in the temple courts") and the small group dynamic ("in their homes"). What do you notice here?

• Check out 2 Timothy 2:2. What insight does it give into the philosophy of small groups?

• Search for the phrase *one another* or *each other* in the New Testament. Of all these commands, which ones can effectively be carried out in big groups? In small groups?

Avoiding an Avoidable Mess

• Remember that small group initiatives can't succeed without competent and trained leaders. A good training resource is the *ReGroup* DVD Curriculum (Zondervan) featuring Henry Cloud, John Townsend, and Bill Donahue. It's not aimed specifically at student ministry, but the principles covered—humorously teaching "groups how to be groups"—apply to every age group.

• Use feedback forms and Web-based evaluations to find out how much your students are taking away from your large-group teaching sessions. Zoomerang (www.zoomerang.com) offers a pretty basic but free Web-based survey service. (A monthly fee applies only if you want to survey more than 50 people.)

• Check out *Moving Forward by Looking Back: Embracing First-Century Practices in Youth Ministry* by Craig Steiner (Zondervan/Youth Specialties, 2009). It proposes a youth ministry modeled after the early church in the book of Acts, and it has some good thoughts on the importance of community.

LOSING YOUR BALANCE

As a collegian, I (Len) attended the one and only gymnastics meet of my life. I was there to watch my classmate Jeannie—a pocket-sized gymnast who'd caused my heart to flip as easily as she catapulted her body all over the arena floor.

But Jeannie isn't what I remember most about that event. She did fine—but the highlight (or lowlight?) was a gymnast from another school. Now I don't want to embarrass this woman—especially if she happens to be a youth director who's now reading this book. So let me just say this plucky little athlete shared the name of a famous Disney character (and I'm not talking about Cruella De Vil or Mary Poppins).

She was a competitor on the balance beam, and I guess it just wasn't her day. She fell off the beam repeatedly—five or six times in all. To her credit, this woman kept hopping back up onto the beam. And to the judges' credit, they graciously gave her about a 5.2. I'm telling you, watching her was painful. And when she finished, I felt exhausted—like I needed to go home and take a 14-hour nap.

I learned three things from that experience: (1) It's cruel to name one's child after an animated character; (2) I'll never be caught walking across a balance beam; and (3) The balance beam is a great metaphor for life.

If you lean too far one way, you can easily take a tumble. Put all your money in stocks and—BAM!—if the market sinks (or should I say when the market sinks!), you're in deep trouble. Let your good work ethic edge toward workaholism and stop taking the time to rest and enjoy life and—BOOM!—you're burned out.

This same balance-beam principle affects youth groups, too. Youth groups can get off-kilter, can lean too far in one direction. You have to monitor things, lest your group slide dangerously toward one extreme or the other. The chart that follows illustrates what I mean:

THE YOUTH GROUP SPECTRUM

ALL FUN, ALL THE TIME	⬌	HYPER-SERIOUS AND STERN
INWARD FOCUSED	⬌	OUTWARD FOCUSED
"SERVE US!"	⬌	SERVICE
LIGHT CONTENT	⬌	HEAVY CONTENT
LOW-COMMITMENT KIDS	⬌	HIGHLY DEVOTED KIDS
KEEP 'EM BUSY AND OUT OF TROUBLE!	⬌	CHALLENGE THEM TO MAKE A DIFFERENCE
ENTERTAINMENT	⬌	GROWTH AND MISSION
"EAT, DRINK, AND BE MERRY"	⬌	"YOU SHALL BE MY WITNESSES"
"LIFE IS ALL ABOUT ME"	⬌	"LIFE IS ALL ABOUT GOD"

I believe a good youth group has a healthy balance of all these characteristics. Good groups are fun as well as purposeful and missional. A well-rounded group offers something for everyone. Just as a good diet pulls from lots of food groups, ensuring that one gets all the vitamins and minerals necessary for good health, our youth ministries need to intentionally program to meet not just the wants of their students, but also their needs. Sometimes the program should feature movie nights and shaving cream fights. And sometimes we need to hit our kids hard with deep, soul-shaking truth and ask them to engage in gut-wrenching ministry.

Every group tends to take on the personality of its leaders. If you're a fun-loving, party-planning, highly social person, then your group will likely mirror those qualities. Your group's activities will constantly edge toward the lighthearted and crazy side. On the contrary, if you're very missional and serious, then over time you may notice that your group could use a dose of lighthearted fun.

All we're saying is be aware of this phenomenon. Monitor it. Every month or so, take a step back and assess the activities of your group. Is there a healthy balance?

Discussion Questions

1. What's the natural bent of your personality? That is, if you tend to get out of balance, which way do you tend to lean?

2. What's wrong with a group that majors on fun times and fellowship together?

3. What's the most significant youth group mission or outreach you've ever been a part of? How did the experience impact the participants?

For Further Study

• Spend some time reflecting on Christ's statement in Matthew 10:39: "Whoever finds their life will lose it, and whoever loses their life for my sake will find it."

• What are the implications of Mark 10:45 for a youth minister? For a youth ministry?

• Try to unpack John 10:10 and how it applies to this whole discussion of balance in youth ministry.

• If you don't already know the Great Commission by heart, take a few minutes to memorize Matthew 28:18-20.

Avoiding an Avoidable Mess

• Every youth group includes both laid-back parents who don't take much of anything too seriously and intense parents who want their kids to graduate from high school with the theological insight of John Piper. Recruit a couple of parents of each type to help you evaluate your ministry. (Just keep in mind that they'll be resistant to ideas that run counter to their natural bent.)

• Visit another youth group or eat lunch with another youth worker and ask, "What's proving effective in your ministry right now?"

• Make a list of the types of youth events you'd probably never plan (not because they're sinful but because they're not your style). Then ask yourself, *Why not?* Pick one and do it anyway.

• Survey your kids. Ask for their honest feedback. What do they like about your group? What would they change and why? Encourage them to be truthful. Sometimes the truth can hurt our feelings, but it can also set us free—right?

MAKING CHANGES TOO QUICKLY

A youth worker who wishes to remain anonymous shares this story:

> Every year, our church holds this big, community-wide holiday extravaganza. It really is amazing and tons of fun—with music, food, festivities for the kids, a silent auction, and the whole deal. This is a *major* social happening—an excellent fund-raiser and a pretty decent outreach all rolled into one. People who've never attended a "religious event" come to this thing. And over the years, a few of them have actually joined our church. This event serves as a showcase for all the talented and hardworking members of our church.
>
> But I'm telling you, this thing has developed a life of its own. It morphed from a good idea into the gigantic tail that wags the dog. It's become all-consuming. For the three months leading up to the event, it completely dominates the church calendar. Then for three months afterward, everyone is pretty much exhausted and catatonic. It even affects the youth group because the students are asked to spend hours and hours helping out.
>
> I guess since I'm the new guy on staff, people feel it's okay to whisper to me about how much they wish we'd stop doing it. I had a guy tell me just the other day, "[The name of the event] has now officially become a sacred cow. The day we stop doing it will be the day we stop taking the Eucharist or having weekly services."
>
> I've been here about seven months now. I witnessed this spectacle shortly after I arrived, and I've experienced firsthand the big toll it takes on everyone. Pretty soon our church will be gearing up to do it again. So I'm wondering, should I say something?

Here's our advice for our well-meaning youth pastor friend: Button your lip. You haven't yet earned the stripes or established the necessary respect or credibility to attempt to lasso such a large sacred cow.

But what you can do is listen to folks patiently (James 1:19). Observe. Praise what's praiseworthy about the event. Be a deliriously happy cheerleader. Roll up your sleeves and help. And as you do, pray that God would open eyes and change hearts—in his perfect timing.

But do not—we repeat—*do not* comment negatively on the event. And by no means should you urge the powers-that-be to reconsider their ways. It's unlikely that such a conversation will go well, and you're not likely to be well received either.

Now, on the other hand, let's say you decide to be bold. Maybe you choose to be prophetic, speaking the truth and even doing so out of love and genuine concern. Just understand that you might very well encounter the same fate of the prophets of old—scorn, anger, persecution, maybe even a rock or two launched in your direction.

Discussion Questions

1. Do you like change or resist it?

2. How can you relate to the story above?

3. What "sacred cows," if any, does your current church (organization) have? Or what programs or events have the potential to become "sacred cows"?

4. Think about a situation in which you were part of an established group and a new leader came and tried to implement a bunch of changes and new initiatives right off the bat. How did you feel?

5. How does a youth worker (often the low person on the proverbial staff totem pole) earn the necessary credibility to become an influential part of the conversation?

6. Come up with a checklist for wise actions to take *before* making changes in established ministry routines or programs.

For Further Study

• Spend some time mulling over the content of 1 Timothy 4:12.

• Ponder Hebrews 13:17. What makes submitting to authority so difficult? Why is submission important to our souls—even when we believe we're right and they're wrong?

• Galatians 6:9 is intriguing. How does it add to your thinking about this subject?

Avoiding an Avoidable Mess

• Instead of spouting off to fellow staff members or volunteers in your ministry, enlist a mature, trustworthy ministry colleague (same gender, similar age, preferably at another local church or ministry) to be your "venting partner." Once a month or so, meet for coffee and let down your hair. Talk honestly about ministry frustrations and other concerns.

Having such a release valve can help you avoid saying too much to people in your own church or group.

• Read the story of Jacob in the book of Genesis (chapters 25 through 49). He was a conniver, a classic control freak who tried to get life to work out the way he believed it should. Only after repeated trials and heartache did he learn to surrender to God—to trust God to work in his way and in his time.

EVENT TRICK AND TRAPS
Consider these real-life youth worker horror stories:

- "I decided to bring in this popular Christian band to do a concert, as they were going to be touring in our part of the country. They gave me two possible dates, and I chose one—a Tuesday night. Safe, right? It was a big deal—lots of money. But I'd been at my church for four years, so the board approved the expense (based on my ticket plan, which would have recouped all our money and maybe even made a little profit). Well, wouldn't you know it? Our two local, rival high schools both made the state basketball playoff semifinals. First time ever! And the game was scheduled for the same night as our concert. Instead of a crowd of 700 or 800, like we expected, we sold fewer than 200 tickets. We ended up losing more than $5,000!"
- "Our group decided to do this combination Easter Egg Hunt/Spring-time Game Day for low-income, at-risk kids. We worked it all out and rented about four buses to pick up the kids. The plan was to bring them back to our church for all kinds of outdoor fun—burgers, softball, soccer, the works. The weather forecast called for a 30 percent chance of rain, but we didn't think anything about it. Well, as we were riding on the buses and bringing the children back to our church, the heavens opened up. I mean, it just started pouring! And it continued to rain for an hour. Our church ball field was a lake. And our gym was being used for a big missions garage sale. We ended up showing the kids a movie in the worship center. And the kids were running around throughout the whole film. It was total chaos! What a mess!"
- "Last October, four hours before we were set to leave for our fall retreat, I got a call that our speaker had a bad case of the flu and wouldn't be joining us. Man! Talk about rocking my world! We scrambled like crazy, and somehow God bailed us out. Different adult leaders jumped in there to save the day. But it was pretty nerve-racking."

The moral of these stories? Always have a Plan B just in case the unexpected happens. If you're planning a big event, find the most anal

"What if?" person on your volunteer team (or in your church) and have her think through everything, imagining every possible worst-case scenario. You may not need to have a contingency plan for an outbreak of Ebola, but you might want a back up plan for what you'd do if the power suddenly went out.

You should also think through the purpose of your events and then assess them afterward. Youth ministry veteran Priscilla Steinmetz uses a chart like this one to evaluate her past events and plan for future ones.

EVENT	PURPOSE	AREA(S) OF GROWTH	RESULT	RATING (1-10)	CHANGE
Back-to-School Bash	Fun, outward growth	Social	Students brought friends and had a good time	8	Check school calendars for event conflicts
Soup Kitchen	Serving, inward growth	Emotional, Spiritual	Students were moved by interacting w/ the homeless	9	Next time take smaller groups— too many cooks in the kitchen (literally)
Valen- tine's Dinner/ Dance	Fun, outward growth	Social	Students w/out dates were isolated; too much PDA control	6	Keep the dinner part and maybe add cos- tumes to the party w/ a theme
Jr. High Retreat	Fun, inward growth, leadership development	All	Senior high students developed skills; stu- dents were challenged in every aspect and had fun	8	Change date to a weekend when stu- dents have no school on Monday; allow more downtime

After listing your events, analyze each one—column by column. First, what was the activity's purpose or goal? Was it just for fun? Was it a means of connecting students and building community? Was it intended to serve others, reach out to unchurched kids, or stimulate internal spiritual maturity? Was it supposed to develop leaders?

Second, what kind of growth did you hope to achieve in your students: Social, cultural, moral, biblical, theological, interpersonal, personal, intellectual?

Third, give a brief summary of what transpired.

Fourth, rate the event on a 1 to 10 scale (with 1 being "Terrible!" and 10 being "Terrific!")

Finally, jot down some notes about what needs to change if you do the event again. Keeping these kinds of notes in a binder can help you as you program in the future.

Discussion Questions

1. How would you rate yourself as a planner? Do you proactively plan for events, or do you tend to react to them?

2. How adept are you at creative problem solving?

3. What would you have done in each of the situations above?

For Further Study

• Spend some time reflecting on Proverbs 22:3, which says: "The prudent see danger and take refuge, but the simple keep going and pay the penalty."

• Read and ponder Proverbs 21:5—"The plans of the diligent lead to profit as surely as haste leads to poverty."

Avoiding an Avoidable Mess

• Turn your vehicle's trunk into a "Youth Ministry Emergency Kit." Include phone numbers, a games book, some Frisbees, a football, some decks of cards, a board game or two, a rope, a kickball or soccer ball, and some sidewalk chalk. You'd be amazed at how many hours you can fill with those few items.

• Keep some crowdbreakers, mixers, or even games on hand (or, even better, in your head) for those occasions when you need to stretch or fill time.

- Every now and then, do a "gut check." Ask yourself, *Why am I doing all these programmed events—really?*

DON'T BE A "VIDEOT"!

In my (Len) first official act as a volunteer youth leader, I showed the movie *Night of the Living Dead* to about 25 junior high students.

I suppose it's possible to have a more disastrous debut—but right now I'm hard-pressed to think what that might look like.

Since the start of school in September, and with the help of a couple of college buddies, I'd been leading a Sunday school class of seventh and eighth graders. Things were going well. We were getting to know our small but rambunctious group of middle schoolers. And maybe we were even helping them grasp a few basic spiritual truths.

Our bigger vision, however, was for a more lively midweek meeting. And since Halloween fell on a Wednesday that year, we decided to use the occasion to make a big splash. How about a costume party with prizes? Agreed. Lots of great homemade snacks? Absolutely! (Let's get those moms involved.) A few games? Definitely.

But we still needed that extra something. Something memorable—something that would get the kids to invite their friends and create a stir on campus. What could it be?

I thought back to some of those old monster movies I'd seen as a kid. Schlocky, campy classics like *Godzilla* or even better—*The Creature from the Black Lagoon* or *The Wolfman*.

Yes. Perfect! We could show an old Bela Lugosi movie.

I'm dating myself here, but these were the days before Blockbuster—and long before Netflix, Blu-rays, and DVDs. VHS technology existed, but it seemed as farfetched as Luke Skywalker's lightsaber. It wasn't yet mainstream. In those

I'd been working for Campus Life full time for just a few months, and I'd been trying to start a club for one of my assigned schools. This involved making weekly trips (about 45 minutes away) in the early afternoon after my seminary classes. I'd head over with my college student volunteer, and we'd spend time on the high school campus and with individual students, have supper in a board member's home, and then lead a Bible study with a group of core, Christian students.

One night hardly anyone showed up—just the host and a few of her friends. Although I'd prepared for the study, I spent most of the time sharing my disappointment over the poor turnout and urging them to invite their friends. We didn't do the study; we may have prayed—I can't remember. But I do remember driving back to seminary and hearing my volunteer say, "At least they came."

"What do you mean?" I responded.

And he said, "Those kids came to the meeting. I don't think it was right to get all over them and dump your frustration on them. I think we should have had our lesson."

He was right, and I was convicted. I'd been meeting my needs and remained oblivious to theirs. Since then, I've always tried to "have the lesson" for whoever shows up, no matter who or how many.

—Dave Veerman

days showing a film meant exactly that—celluloid on a reel, an old movie projector clicking away. It meant students holding up their fingers to make shadow animals (and obscene gestures) on the screen.

On the morning of our big event, I just knew we were on the verge of something great. We had good buzz. Lots of kids were planning to come. And then it hit me: I'd done everything—except secure my monster movie! I dashed over to the one place in town where you could actually rent movies and breathlessly told the clerk about our plans. He grimaced.

"It's Halloween, man. Everything I've got like that is already rented out."

One by one I began listing potential films.

After each suggestion, he shook his head. With each rejection I felt like the disorganized goof that I was.

Finally, he brightened, "Wait—I do have one movie back there that would work perfectly for you. What about *Night of the Living Dead*?"

A devout Baptist, I'd never heard of it, much less seen it.

"What's it like?"

"Oh, zombies and stupid stuff. It's great. They'll love it."

"It's not *overly* scary, right?"

"Nah, man, it's really cheesy. They'll love it."

So, I rented it. And that's the movie we ignorantly threaded into our Bell & Howell projector at about 6:55 p.m. on October 31, 1979.

At 7:20, as the junior high girls began to shake and sob hysterically and the boys hooted in bloodthirsty delight, I had a moment of theological clarity: *I am in major trouble*. As far as I knew, there was no existing universal set of standards for what should be done at an inaugural youth ministry function. But if there were, I'm pretty sure graphic depictions of cannibalism wouldn't have been on the list.

I pulled my wide-eyed friend Steve to the side. "The guy at the movie place told me this was 'cheesy,' not scary. It's a horror film!" I hissed. "We've got to pull the plug!"

"We can't," he said, his eyes still riveted to the screen, "All the boys are *totally* into it. If we turn it off, they'll mutiny. They'll never come back."

Long pause, punctuated by more ear-piercing screams from across the room. "Okay, what if we stop the projector—just for a minute. I can give a little speech: 'Remember, kids, this is *just a movie*. These are actors. It's not real blood.' We'll calm everybody down. And then we can...um...give everyone the option of watching the movie, or they can...go upstairs and play games."

"Okay," Steve mumbled, still transfixed by the flickering images. "How 'bout I stay down here with the movie group?"

So that's what we did. Steve and the boys all elected to finish the flick—every last gory minute of it. Meanwhile, the girls and I spent the rest of our "fun party" in another room. As I recall, that consisted of a very long hour spent listening to sniffling, trying to reassure, attempting to change the subject, trying to be lighthearted and silly, and praying that God would erase those gruesome images from their young brains. I dreaded the phone calls that would surely come the next day. But I took comfort in the fact that since I was only a volunteer, at least I'd experience no financial repercussions.

Discussion Questions

1. Caught in the situation described above, what would you do?

2. How might all this trouble have been avoided?

3. What's the best use of video you've ever seen in a worship service or youth gathering? What's the worst?

For Further Study

• Read and reflect on Philippians 4:8. It provides a good, concise framework for thinking through whether a film or clip is appropriate for youth group viewing.

• The words of the apostle Paul to the Christians at Ephesus are worth our consideration: "Be very careful, then, how you live—not as unwise but as wise, making the most of every opportunity, because the days are evil" (Ephesians 5:15-16). If we have only a very limited amount of exposure to our students each week, then what are the implications for how we should utilize those moments? And how often should we rely on video?

Avoiding an Avoidable Mess
WISE RULES
- Don't overuse video.
- Make sure you have an updated license to show videos to your group. Talk to the administrator of your church or ministry, or check out http://www.cvli.com—the Web site of Christian Video Licensing International, a company that works with churches to ensure they're compliant with all copyright laws.
- Surf over to the Church Copyright Association (http://www.churchca.com) for professional, expert help with questions about what's legal and what isn't.
- Always, always, *always* preview the video! When you do so, try to evaluate movies through different eyes: From the perspective of that sheltered, home-schooled kid; with the mindset of that hyper-conservative mom or dad. Whatever makes your eyes widen will probably make some parents' eyes pop out of their heads!
- Let a parent volunteer (or members of your parent advisory team) know of your plans.
- Expect some backlash. Parents are all over the map on this issue. While many let their kids watch just about anything, others suspect anything that comes out of Hollywood.
- Just because you don't hear any complaints, that doesn't mean everyone is fine with your decision.

8

DEALING WITH AUTHORITIES

"I just want to reach kids!" the youth worker exclaimed. "And all this other junk keeps getting in the way." With that, he tossed his ministry report forms into the air.

Schedules, meetings, reports, rules, and regulations—we can get tired of the busywork that tends to clutter our schedules. All we want to do is hang out with students and plan and lead their activities. Yet someone (often, our supervisor) always seems to get in the way with another agenda—always tells us what to do.

No wonder youth leaders often resist those in authority.

Yet living under authority is a fact of life—check out the Roman soldier's comment to Jesus in Matthew 8:5-13. Having a boss comes with the territory. So we labor under senior pastors, church boards, supervisors, executive directors, and so forth—and sometimes we chafe under their leadership and direction.

And even if we never run into a single problem with the folks in charge of our church or organization, then we must interact every day with those who have authority over the students we're trying to reach—parents, school officials, coaches, and others in the community at large, including members of law enforcement.

If we truly want to be effective in youth ministry, we'll need to learn how to deal with authorities.

WINNING OVER THE SENIOR PASTOR

If you work in a local church, the first significant authority figure with whom you'll have to deal is the senior pastor. (If you're in a parachurch organization, think "director.")

Les Christie tells this story of an early ministry experience:

> During a youth group all-nighter, I organized a Polaroid camera scavenger hunt. (Today, you'd use a digital camera.) Each carload of adults and kids got a Polaroid camera and a list of pictures to take. The lists of

pictures required certain situations, such as sitting in a police car and being stuffed into a Laundromat clothes dryer. You know, *fun* stuff.

I had our guest speaker and four high school students in my care. It was 1:00 a.m., and we'd just finished taking a picture of our group crammed into one of those old-fashioned telephone booths. Now we were in a K-Mart parking lot to get a picture of the students on a mechanical horsey ride, when two police cars arrived with their lights flashing.

The police asked who was in charge. When I stepped forward, they leaned me against a police car and frisked me. The kids and our guest speaker were lined up against a wall. Three more police cars arrived from neighboring districts. Now I'm worried, and I'm explaining to an officer who we are and what we're doing.

The officer then informed me that a neighbor had seen a flash of light and called the police to report that some kids had blown up the telephone booth. I knew it had simply been the camera flash. But it just so happened that the week before, someone had actually blown up a telephone booth in that area. The police were taking no chances.

I asked them to call the senior pastor to verify my identity. So an officer called Ben—remember, it's 1:00 a.m.—and explained the situation.

Ben said, "I've never heard of the guy," and hung up.

Things got pretty sticky after that. I was finally set free when the police drove by the telephone booth and confirmed that it had not, in fact, exploded.

Senior pastors can make or break your youth ministry. I worked 22 years with Ben and valued every minute of our time together. And I did get him back—but that's another story.

Let's underline that important phrase: "Senior pastors can make or break your youth ministry." If you gather a group of veteran youth workers in a room and ask about their "senior pastor moments," you'll get an earful. Tyrants. Control freaks. Lousy managers. Always taking the parents' side. But you'll also hear positive comments. Caring. A mentor. My advocate with parents and the board. Understanding and supportive.

The difference in the two kinds of senior pastors may be due to personality type, spiritual depth, ministry experience, or something else. But regardless of your senior pastor's makeup, getting to know (and learning to get along with) him is vitally important.

Sometimes that's easier said than done. We need to approach our supervising pastor with care, while remembering the following points:

1. Most senior pastors, like school administrators, don't want to hear negative reports from parents. Will they ever receive negative reports?

Idealism is great, but it can cause problems, too. Take the newly graduated youth worker who believes working for a Christian organization will be heaven on earth. She'll soon hit the rude reality that the organization is composed of sinful, fallible people with their own strengths and weaknesses, pet peeves and idiosyncrasies, and good and bad days, Or consider the stressed-out, overburdened, do-it-alone minister who knows that sharing the load with another leader would certainly be better than this. So an associate is hired—and with this new person comes the necessity to plan, schedule, communicate, resolve conflict, and manage. The ministry becomes complicated in a hurry.

Of course. We're not perfect, so we'll make mistakes. But that makes it even more important that we communicate well with parents (see chapter 6) and let the senior pastor know that we're working hard on those relationships.

2. Most senior pastors—especially those who've virtually worked alone in the ministry for some time (such as church planters)—are not good managers of people. In other words, they're not adept at affirming staff, matching job descriptions with a person's gifts, and holding regular performance reviews. Therefore, we shouldn't expect them to be effective executives, and we need to be self-starters. This issue is probably the most frequent complaint of youth workers about their senior pastors.

3. Most senior pastors, especially in the early days of the youth minister's employment, believe in the youth minister and want him to succeed. We should use this honeymoon period to gain the senior pastor's trust and establish regular communication channels with him.

4. Most senior pastors will protect and defend staff members in whom they believe and trust. This means we need to work hard at building that belief and trust by communicating regularly and sharing stories of changed lives. We also need to see youth ministry as a part of the larger church—not a separate organization within the church that's competing for resources.

5. Most senior pastors want to fully fund responsible and effective youth ministry, but they don't want to waste money. They know financial resources are in short supply, and they want to be good stewards. So we need to budget carefully, be prepared to defend each item in the budget, and spend wisely.

Recently, a veteran youth worker remarked,

> When I started in youth ministry, I jumped in with both feet, full of enthusiasm and energy—spending time with students and planning exciting events and activities. I hated anything that kept me from kids: Staff meetings, ministry plans and reports, and even staff social events. I got the reputation of being arrogant and aloof—a loner and not a team player. I wish I knew then that the respect and support of the senior pastor (and other staff) was vital to the success of the ministry.

Discussion Questions

1. Who are your supervisors in ministry?

2. In what ways does your ministry differ now from when you were hired (expectations, work environment, resources, freedom, and so on)?

3. What can you do to improve your relationship with your senior pastor or organizational director?

For Further Study

• Meditate on Hebrews 13:17 and 1 Peter 5:5, considering how these passages apply to your relationship with your supervisor or senior pastor.

• Talk with other youth pastors in the area and ask for tips on how to work most effectively within a larger staff.

Avoiding an Avoidable Mess

• At the beginning of every week, let your superior know your schedule and what you hope to accomplish that week.

As far as bosses go, I've had an assortment. A while back I had one boss for whom I had zero respect. We didn't really have any kind of relationship, so there was no attempt on his part to maintain anything. He was just there. I guess it wasn't horrible, but it sure wasn't good.

At another place I had a better situation. My boss never micromanaged me. He gave me a lot of freedom, and I tried to respect that. I would run stuff—ideas and issues—by him and keep him in the loop. I wanted him to know what was going on. Anytime I had the opportunity to do stuff with him or for him—preach, lead confirmation classes— I tried to do that to build his trust. We didn't hang out or socialize much. He didn't initiate that sort of thing, and I tried not to have those expectations. But we'd go to lunch about once a month or so. I'd often initiate and he was receptive. We even went fishing once. He wasn't overinvolved, but he was involved enough to show he cared. And I didn't go in and moan to him. If I were going to talk with him, I'd have a reason.

Can I say he was a mentor figure? No. But I don't know that our relationship needed to be like that. I had to realize it wasn't going to be that way, and that was okay. There were other people with whom I could pursue that kind of relationship.

—Alan Johnson

• Don't wait for your superior to set up an appointment for a performance review. Take the initiative.

WORKING WITH CHURCH BOARDS

Mark Oestreicher tells this story about a time when he ignored a problem, hoping it would just go away:

> The church board had made a ridiculous request of me—wanting a formal written report about a personal issue that had no effect on my ministry. Truthfully, they were out of line in asking. But I should have done one of two things: I should have given them the report, or I should have respectfully informed them where they could put their request. But I chose to be passive-aggressive and to ignore them. Bad choice. A year later they fired me.

Mark's failure to respond to the church board cost him his job.

All ministries have boards that are usually made up of laypeople charged with some oversight responsibilities. Each Youth for Christ chapter has a "board of directors"; Young Life chapters have "committees"; churches have boards of "deacons," "elders," "trustees," or something similar. While the senior pastor or director is the "boss," she's usually accountable to one of these collections of overseers. And depending on the chain of command in your organization, there may be situations in which you report directly to one of these boards.

Getting along with the men and women in authority over us only makes sense. And we can do quite a bit to improve our relationships with board members. (As a caveat, let us stress that any direct contact you have with the board should be done with the approval of the senior pastor—never behind her back.)

Here are some ways we can improve our relationship with board members:

- Greet them warmly at church and other venues (don't avoid them). They should see you as a friend, not a stranger or adversary.
- Get together with board members one-on-one for fellowship and input.
- Ask for their help and suggestions for the ministry (as a group and individually). If possible, the requests should be specific. For example, we could ask for their help in teaching about the Bible or a specific topic, for their ideas on how to better deal with parents, or for something similar.
- Find a key board member to mentor you or to serve as a ministry volunteer. This person could help interpret you to the board and vice versa.

These actions take some careful thought. But investments in this area can pay huge dividends for your ministry.

Discussion Questions

1. What boards or committees have some degree of oversight of your ministry?

2. What key people should you work at getting to know better? What can you do to communicate better with them about the ministry? In what ways might the senior pastor or executive director help you in this process?

For Further Study

- Reflect on Acts 15:1-35, the story of the Jerusalem Council (Paul's "board"). Consider Paul's approach at the council, James' actions, and what you can learn about staff-board relations.

Early in my ministry, I served in a large church, and the elders were deciding about a huge building project. I knew most of them weren't in favor of going forward without having financial pledges to cover the whole amount (about half of what we needed had been pledged to that point)— and that made a lot of sense to me. But after a long meeting with the senior pastor, they voted unanimously to proceed. I was ticked off, especially because the elders didn't have the courage of their convictions, not to mention the fact that the decision was fiscally irresponsible, and on and on! And I shared my feelings with a few of those church leaders.

Not long after, I realized how foolishly and impetuously I'd acted and that I easily could have been bounced from my position. I hadn't been in that meeting. I hadn't been privy to all the facts. I should have trusted that these godly people were sincerely trying to follow God's lead. Fortunately, the elders to whom I'd unloaded were gracious and patient with me (probably taking into account my age and experience), and they didn't get mad or get even. So I continued to serve in that place.

If I knew then what I know now (having worked with several elder boards since then), I would have listened more, spoken less, and shown more trust.

—*Christopher Ribaudo*

• Get a copy of the by-laws of your church or organization and refresh your memory on how your church, denomination, or ministry is organized. Consider the formal and informal chains of command.

Avoiding an Avoidable Mess
• Don't get into the habit of thinking (or even worse, saying), *What do they know? They're out of touch.* Approach board members individually and as a group with respect, remaining open to their thoughts, ideas, and opinions.

• Outline a strategy for communicating effectively with the boards, including your ministry philosophy and reports of ministry results. Do this with the senior pastor's approval.

SECRETARIES RULE!
If you were to chart out the official power structure of the average church or ministry organization, the church secretary (or office manager or administrative assistant) might seem to have very little authority. But anyone who's spent much time working in a ministry setting knows church secretaries wield a great deal of power within any congregation. If I knew then what I know now, I'd recognize how important it is to have a good working relationship with the church secretary.

Let's take a quick look at the kinds of power and influence a church secretary holds.

First and foremost, secretaries are the door-keepers—most everything from the outside comes through them. Consider how secretaries can affect the ministry simply by the way they relate to parents and others who call in (or stop in) with their questions and comments.

Most secretaries know the ins and outs of the church and how it works—especially if they've been there for a few years. That can include everything from the location of supplies and the proper procedures for signing out the church van, to the inside politics of congregational life and how things *really* get done. (Think "Radar" from *M*A*S*H*.)

Having the church secretary on your side only makes sense. If church secretaries doubt our competency, spirituality, or commitment, or if they believe we're arrogant or irresponsible, then they can become formidable adversaries. Some youth workers have learned this lesson too late.

Consider the differences between these two phone calls:

ADVERSARY SECRETARY
Secretary: Hello, First Church.
Caller: Is [name of youth minister] in? I'd like to speak with her.
Secretary: I doubt it. She usually can't get out of bed until 11 or so!

ALLY SECRETARY
Caller: Hi. Is [name of youth minister] there?
Secretary: No, not yet. I believe she's on a ministry appointment near the high school. She spends so much time with kids—what a worker!

> With this key person as an ally, we can learn with whom we should talk when we need something, personal quirks of the other church leaders, how to prepare a budget request, and other inside information. And the secretary can also be an effective PR person for your ministry—with parents and anyone else who calls.
>
> Here are a few tips for making the church secretary your friend. (We'll use feminine pronouns for this list—although the number of men working as church secretaries or office managers has been increasing.)

- Treat her like a friend. Be pleasant and cordial and show genuine interest in her family and interests.
- Keep your schedule and word. She needs to know you are reliable, punctual, and trustworthy.
- Give her what she needs when she needs it. For example, if you want the secretary to make calls, send emails, or put together a flier, then give her the request and provide the necessary information early enough that she can plan *her* schedule and not feel pressured or panicked. Submit your facilities or equipment request forms the right way. And be sure to include receipts with your expense reports.
- Leave her office supplies alone. (Get your own.)
- Inform her of your schedule so she can give the correct message and won't feel foolish when people are trying to contact you. When you

leave for lunch, for example, you could say, "I have a lunch appoint-ment with [person—you can be as specific as you want], and I should be back at [time]." If your schedule changes drastically (for example, you'll be an hour late), then call and let her know.

- Share ministry stories—especially amazing activities and changed lives—and struggles. Ask her to pray for you and specific ministry needs, letting her know she's on your team.
- Celebrate her presence. This includes thanking her for her work, bringing her treats, praying together, remembering her birthday, and so forth.
- Remember—secretaries rule! (And they often rock!)

Discussion Questions

1. What do you know about the church (or ministry) secretary? What does the secretary know about you?

2. In what ways might the secretary enhance the ministry?

3. What can you do to improve your relationship with your secretary?

For Further Study

• Too often we treat secretaries and other support staff as invisible. But they play invaluable roles in the ministry. Consider how you can thank them for what they do.

• Meditate on the "little people" who are mentioned in the Bible who had a major impact. For example, we know Paul had a secretary, even though we don't know that person's name.

Avoiding an Avoidable Mess

• Make a big deal about National Administrative Assistants Day.

• Begin to implement some or all of the suggested action steps above.

MAKING EDUCATORS YOUR ALLIES

Just like students and their parents, educators—teachers, school adminis-trators, and staff members—come in all shapes, sizes, personalities, and temperaments. Some may feel threatened by our ministry, assuming we're trying to undermine their authority or contradict their teachings. Some may aggressively oppose us because of their personal religious (or antireligious) beliefs. Some may question our involvement, especially in and around the school, because of their understanding of the idea of the "separation of church and state." And some may seem intimidating to us simply because of their position (for example, principal, assistant principal, athletic director, and so forth) or because we recall painful incidents during *our own* student days with a person holding that title.

While some school staff members may seem wary of our efforts, most schools will also have staff members who appreciate what we're trying to do. Most educators care deeply for their students and will support anyone who is honest, open, and seeking to help kids. Plus the staff of most schools will usually include quite a few committed Christians who want to do what they can to help our ministries.

As I (Dave) look back over my ministry years with Campus Life, educators of both types stand out. Here are just a few of the folks I can recall.

- The high school assistant principal who denied me access to the campus with the phrase, "If we let you, then we'll have to let the Boy Scouts and everyone else." I've never been sure why he feared the Boy Scouts. Actually, he *wouldn't* have had to let "everyone else"—that was just a convenient excuse.
- The principal who said I needed to get approval from the school board. (So I did.)
- The assistant principal who sought to compliment me by saying, "I've never had a negative comment about Campus Life." I thanked him but thought, *I could be dead, and they'd have no negative comments either*.
- The principal who said, "Look, we need all the help we can get around here," and then proceeded to give me a green light, along with the guidelines.

Regardless of how much time a youth worker wants to spend at a school, he or she needs to

If you ever wonder why principals and other educators might seem suspicious of your motives, remember that *many outsiders* would like to use the school—businesses for marketing and sales, employers for cheap labor, politicians for voters, religious groups for converts, service clubs for members, the armed forces for recruits, and more. (Add to this list the drug dealers, gang leaders, and others who lurk at the fringes of the campus.) Sorting out the positive and legitimate from the negative and nefarious can be difficult and time-consuming. Saying "no" is much easier.

see the educators who work there as potential allies. We're not at war with them; instead, we need to work with them whenever we can.

I also remember these events and opportunities:

- The small group of Christian teachers with whom I met weekly for prayer (in one of their classrooms).
- The district superintendent (a believer) who gave me a pass to all the district's athletic events.
- The high school principal who pulled me aside at school one day and asked what I thought he should do about a local youth pastor who wanted to come on campus from time to time to have lunch with students from his church.
- Football coaches who asked our staff members to serve as team chaplains.
- The many teachers who invited me and other staff members into their classes to speak on everything from Intelligent Design to dealing with death.
- The high school principal who attended a memorial in honor of Mike O'Hara, our Campus Life staff member for the school (he died of cancer) and wept as he recounted Mike's impact on his life and his students.

Through the years, I've been privileged to sponsor dozens of high school assemblies, to speak at baccalaureate services, to present seminars at gatherings of student councils, to address PTA groups, to lecture in classes, to lead competitive homecoming events for the student body, and many other opportunities. And I know youth workers who regularly chaperone school ski clubs, band trips, and cheerleading squads. Others have worked on the sidelines at football games, served refreshments at school events, advised the yearbook staff, helped coach an athletic team, or simply swept the floors during halftime at basketball games. All these activities provided access to kids and opportunities for building relationships with them.

Ideally, educators will see us as helpful, valuable resources who are willing to serve with no hidden agendas. But, to be honest, winning their trust and cooperation takes time. Here's how:

Begin by setting up an appointment to meet with the school principal. Dress nicely, be friendly, act professionally, and be open. Introduce yourself and let this person know what you're about, including your background and information about who you represent. Don't hide the fact that you represent a Christian organization or group but avoid using religious jargon. Explain that several kids from your group go to this school, so this person will probably see you at various school events (where the public has access and is welcome) and in the community. Also explain why you are in youth work—your concern and care for students—and that you want to be of help wherever you can.

Answer any questions and then express your gratitude for this person's time and work with students. Then leave—this appointment shouldn't be long. And leave your business card behind for future contact.

During the school year, follow any guidelines the school has given you about what you may or may not do on school property. Principals and school districts vary greatly on this; some allow almost total access, while others keep the campus off limits.

Be visible. Ideally the administration, coaches, teachers, and others should see you doing just what you promised: Building relationships with students and being a positive role model.

Be friendly and respectful. This means smiling and greeting the educators you've met and introducing yourself to those you haven't. Just as you do with students, work hard at remembering their names.

Be helpful. This includes offering your services in some of the ways mentioned above. Schools are almost always looking for help and volunteer support with clubs and teams.

Be appreciative. When you see news stories about the school, an educator, or a student being honored, drop the principal and those involved a congratulatory note and express thanks for their hard work. Encourage parents to do the same. School administrators usually hear only the complaints. So they love getting compliments once in a while.

At the end of the year, schedule another brief appointment with the principal. Express your thanks for her help and ask for feedback

It was easy and sometimes tempting to see teachers and administrators in the local schools as the enemy. Yet looking back, I can see that brief conversations and relationships that developed with school personnel were of great value. If I could do it over, I would have been more intentional about knowing and relating to the people who spent a lot more time with the students in my group than I did.

I'll never forget the principal who called me into his office because he was at his wit's end about a sudden epidemic of interest in satanic symbols and power among his students. As a nominally religious guy, he said he believed in the Devil theoretically, but he was beginning to wonder if there was more to this area than he was prepared to deal with. He wanted to talk with "someone more familiar with these things." Hmmm.

If I could run the instant replay, I would have presented myself more often as a fellow adult to teachers and administrators. Mostly they knew me only in my role as a local youth director. But when I joined the Kiwanis club, they began to see me and treat me as someone they knew in a different category than just one of many outsiders who might potentially cause trouble on campus.

I would have paid closer attention to what my youth group kids said about specific teachers. I quoted C. S. Lewis so often in my conversations and talk-tos with the group that several of them ended up writing papers for the AP English teacher at one high school in town. Eventually, one of my students told me this teacher wanted to see me after school. When we met, he told me he wondered at first why he was getting so many papers that quoted Lewis or were reports on some of his books. He said, "I knew the name, of course, but I'd never actually read Lewis. So I picked up *Mere Christianity* last summer. It changed my life."

Mostly, I would have been more deliberate about watching for ways to be seen as the ally of teachers and principals. I would have practiced being for them what I hoped they would be for me. In hindsight, good relationships with the adults who oversaw a great deal of the lives of my students were never a waste of time or effort. They paid off so handsomely that I wonder now why I didn't do more of that!
—*Neil Wilson*

on how you did at living within the stated rules and guidelines. This would be a good time to ask for suggestions and to offer to help even more next year.

If you're working in a local congregation, you may be thinking: *My group draws students from a dozen schools. There's no way can I be that involved in all of those schools!*

That may be true—but if you *could* be this involved, would you? If you can honestly answer yes, then why not design a strategy with your staff for covering the schools you can? Building strong relationships with educators can open doors and help you reach kids.

Discussion Questions

1. Think of the school where the largest number of your students attend. What's the principal's name? How many times a week.is someone from your staff on campus there?

2. What Christian educators do you know? What can you do *with them* to reach kids?

3. In what ways could you and your staff get involved on local junior high and high school campuses?

For Further Study

• Spend some time reflecting on Paul's Mars Hill experience (Acts 17:16-34) and how it relates to youth ministry.

• Meditate on 1 Corinthians 9:21-22.

• If you work in a church, contact a local Young Life or Youth for Christ director and have her talk with you about how to work with public school students in and around their schools.

Avoiding an Avoidable Mess

• Ask a Christian teacher and a Christian administrator to talk with your staff about church and state issues.

• Have a Christian coach or choir or band director visit the staff meeting and share how faith impacts his work with students.

STAYING WITHIN THE LAW

Consider the following true confessions of youth ministry run-ins with the law that were collected on the Youth Specialties Web site:

- *Indecent Exposure*: "We were at a resort in Wisconsin, and three of my students were mooning people out of the hotel window. Security and police were called. Fun night!"
- *Simple Kidnapping*: "We were playing a game of kidnapped with one group of kids outside the church. We were guarding the 'hostage.' Another group had to sneak up and release the hostage. It was after midnight, and a neighbor called the cops on us."
- *Prowler*: "An office worker saw me and three others attempting to climb the church with a grappling hook."
- *Code 8 Fire Alarm*: "We were putting on a labyrinth during a lock-in for the senior high. A candle fell over and set the pulpit on fire in the sanctuary—20-foot flames and $200,000 in damage, four weeks before Easter: Police and 10 fire trucks."
- *Suspicious Persons*: "Going home from summer camp, we stopped at a mall. About four of our senior high guys had Power Ranger masks on and plastic ninja knives. They were running through the mall and stores, harassing 'customers' (our youth group). The authorities were not amused."
- *Oops!*: "We spent the night in the church parking lot in cardboard boxes, in order to simulate a homeless village. The senior pastor called the police."

If we could interview these youth workers, each one would probably say something like this: "If I knew then what I know now, I would have thought about how our actions would affect the community and how the police might respond. I would have better anticipated the possible implications of what we were planning to do."

We may chuckle at some of the incidents above, but dealing with law enforcement is no laughing matter. We know that breaking a law, or even appearing to do so, is serious and can destroy a ministry and a life. Even accusations that are eventually proven to be false, totally bogus, and thrown out of court can stain a reputation and follow a person for the rest of his or her life. So why are we sometimes so careless in this area?

Perhaps we believe we're above the law—it's a stupid law anyway, we think, so we don't have to obey it! While very few youth workers would admit to having this attitude, many act this way—like when we break curfew or ignore speed limits in certain areas.

Maybe we figure we'll make an exception and, just this once, do what we know is wrong—like stuffing a van or bus with way too many kids.

Or maybe some of us enjoy the risk and get a thrill from getting away with something—such as stealing a unique traffic sign or going with kids to trash a rival school's football field.

And some of us may think it's no big deal, or we rationalize our actions—for example, illegally copying a DVD or music.

In most cases, however, I believe the truth is that youth workers probably just don't think about it. That comes with being young—you're idealistic, you feel invincible, and you have limited life experience. (And that fits right in with the purpose of this book: To help less-experienced youth workers learn from *others'* experiences.)

So, how can you avoid embarrassing situations similar to the ones described above? You should...

- Always think through the legal implications of your actions and activities.
- Avoid sponsoring, sanctioning, or approving *anything* you know is illegal. (If you aren't sure about some activity's legality, ask a lawyer or police officer.)
- Let parents and kids know about this policy.
- Inform the relevant authorities—including your senior pastor or supervisor—when you think something you and the group will be doing may *appear* to be wrong. (Informing the neighbors might also be good.)
- Don't let your ministry crash and burn over something immature, silly, and irresponsible. Remember that you are a role model for these kids—and willfully breaking the law sets a terrible—and unbiblical—example.

Discussion Questions

1. In what aspects of youth ministry are you the most tempted to break the law?

2. What might happen if you and your youth group hit the news as being busted, arrested, or investigated?

3. What changes should you make in your ministry philosophy and style to make sure you operate within the law?

For Further Study
• Spend some time reflecting on Jesus' answer to the Pharisees about taxes and Caesar in Matthew 22:15-22. Consider how this biblical principle relates to youth ministry.

• Meditate on Romans 13:5 and 1 Peter 2:13-14.

• Buy copies of Jack Crabtree's *Better Safe Than Sued: Keeping Your Students and Ministry Alive* (Zondervan/Youth Specialties, 2008) and read and discuss the book with your staff.

Avoiding an Avoidable Mess
• Talk with your staff about the most common areas of potential law violation within youth ministry—such as traffic laws, curfew, copyright, and so forth. Decide how you'll avoid breaking those laws.

• Think through other potential sticky situations, including everything from behavior that simply *appears* to break the law to very serious violations such as physical and sexual abuse. Consider what you could do to prevent those predicaments.

• Inform your students and parents at the beginning of the year (when you're giving the ministry overview) of the "no law-breaking policy" and what it includes.

MONEY MATTERS

WILD GOOSE CHASE!!! screamed the headline on the flier, and that's what we'd deliver. As the head honcho of this big event, I (Dave) outlined a plan that would send a bus to each high school involved to pick up students and transport them throughout the suburbs. Beginning with an initial clue, the kids from each school would move from place to place and clue to clue until they converged on the location of a real live goose, which they would actually chase and, hopefully, catch. We expected hundreds of students in our Campus Life chapter to participate.

Everything was set, including the budget. For just a few bucks, a high school student could have a great time chasing the elusive goose and then gather with everyone else for an exciting program.

And the event went off without a hitch—until afterward when I began tabulating the income and expenses. That's when I discovered a fatal flaw in my budget. When computing the cost of the buses (by far our largest expenditure) *per student*, I'd based my numbers on *full buses*. In other words, if a bus cost $100 to rent for the evening and would hold 50 students—then that bus would cost, according to my calculations, $2 a student. So that's the amount I added to our other expenses to determine the ticket price.

That reasoning seemed sound, except for one detail—we'd break even on the buses only if every one of them was full. In reality, while a few schools hit the maximum that evening, most were way under—with a few sending only about 5 to 10 students each. So with 15 buses in play, you imagine the result.

We lost our shirts! And I was in big trouble.

Fortunately, we were able to negotiate with the bus company for a lower amount. But I learned a valuable lesson—a lesson that was reinforced, I must add, by my boss.

A fact of life (and of ministry) is that everything has a cost: Buses, food, office equipment, sound systems, desks, computers, hired talent, supplies, Bibles, snacks, phones, pens, paper...and salaries! And that money has to come from somewhere. So, whether we like it or not, money—and managing it—plays a vital role in youth ministry.

PLANNING A MINISTRY BUDGET

Can you believe that I (Len) worked for several years at one affluent church and never once had to turn in a budget? Beg for bucks? Are you kidding? Lobby the elders and trustees for ministry funding? No way! The unwritten rule was, "Do anything within reason, turn in your receipts, and we'll pay for it." Pretty sweet deal—but extremely rare. And probably not the best way to operate.

In fact, a policy like that can lead even an experienced youth worker into spending irresponsibly or, at the very least, not appreciating what the ministry actually costs.

At most churches (including the one where I'm working now), the rules for ministry budgeting are quite explicit and almost always in writing. We have a clear process. Even if your church or ministry doesn't have clearly stated budgeting policies and procedures, careful budgeting is still important. Here's why:

A budget will help you determine spending priorities and spend accordingly. Regardless of the financial resources of the institution, the amount of money available is finite, and you'll have a spending limit. Do you really want to spend so much on meeting snacks and so little on Bibles? Do you want to get to the end of the year and discover that you have nothing left for camp scholarships? How we use resources (emotion, time, energy, and money) reveals our values. Wouldn't it be better to plan on investing in those aspects of the ministry that you consider to be invaluable and nonnegotiable?

A budget will help you discover (uncover) the real costs. That's not exactly true, of course, because a budget is a plan, a spending guide. But putting together a budget requires that we consider both possible expenses and sources of income. Then, when we see the actual records of money taken in and spent, we'll see how accurate the budget was and be able to plan better the next time.

A budget can serve as a police officer and help you control spending. As you proceed through a ministry year and compare actual expenses to your plan, you can make adjustments. If you find you're spending too much in one area, then you can slow down, change your budget priorities, or look for new funding sources. A budget, along with good record keeping, will help you make informed, responsible decisions.

A budget will help you take stewardship seriously. God tells us to be good stewards of the resources he entrusts to our care. If we don't know how we're using those resources—spending them—then we won't know whether or not we are, in fact, "good and faithful servants" (see Matthew 25:14-30).

Of course, simply designing a financial plan for ministry isn't enough; we must work the plan. This means checking the figures monthly to see if we're on track (see "police officer" above). Even if we're in a situation where our superior gives us tons of freedom in terms of ministry finances, we need to discipline ourselves.

A budget works a lot like a diet. The diet will succeed only if the dieter is disciplined and follows it. Rationalizations won't cut it. And ignorance may be bliss, but it won't absolve us of our responsibility.

Right now you may be thinking of all the reasons against putting together ministry budgets. In case you might forget one, here are some of the more popular excuses (and some answers):

- God called me to reach teenagers, not to do paperwork! (True, but budgets can help you be more effective in reaching teenagers—honest.)
- I'm terrible at math—numbers just confuse me. (Then find someone to do the number crunching for you.)
- I really don't have time for that kind of busy work. (Okay…but you probably know someone who does have the time—and who likes it. Enlist that person's help.)
- All this talk about money disgusts me. Salvation is free, and the ministry should be, too. (Wait a minute, salvation isn't free—remember the cross! Everything we do in ministry costs something; the question isn't whether there's a cost but who will pay the bills.)

Hopefully you caught an important point in a couple of the answers above: Someone else can take this responsibility off your shoulders. That is, you can recruit an accountant-type who loves students to be your official bean counter. What a great way to serve the Lord.

One final thought: We need budgets (plural)—an annual budget for the ministry as a whole, as well as a specific budget for each ministry event that passes an expense threshold determined by the church or organization (for example, a fall retreat, the Christmas party, the annual ski trip, a summer mission trip, and so forth).

One veteran youth worker (who wants to remain anonymous) writes, "My first year in ministry, I overspent my budget by 300 percent. And I nearly got fired. Worse, I never lived down the reputation (with the staff and other church leaders) as a reckless, self-centered spendthrift. If I had known then what I know now, I would have worked out a reasonable budget plan with my senior pastor and then stuck to it."

Discussion Questions

1. What guidelines does your church or organization follow in establishing ministry budgets? When are annual budgets due?

2. What policies are in place regarding fund-raisers, designated gifts, and so on?

3. How are your personal finances? What does your personal or family budget look like? What would those who know you best say about how you handle money?

For Further Study

• Spend some time reflecting on Proverbs 20:18—why it's wise to get advice when making plans.

• If you have a tendency to do rushed, last-minute planning, reflect on the counsel of Proverbs 21:5.

Avoiding an Avoidable Mess

• If your church or ministry has any kind of written policy regarding budget procedures, make sure you get a copy and read it carefully.

• If you have questions or are unclear about any matters related to finances, make an appointment with your supervisor to get the answers and direction you need.

• If dealing with monetary issues is not your strength, see if you can find a gifted parent or other volunteer who will help you with ministry budget planning.

BEING FRUGAL WITH GOD'S RESOURCES

For many years, while I (Dave) was working as Campus Life director for the local area, my home church was struggling with its youth ministry efforts. We ran through a number of youth directors, each with varying degrees of success. So, as you might imagine, church leaders and parents were understandably excited when the youth group began to grow.

The new director was young, charismatic, and talented; and he and his "cool" friends put on quite a show. Every Tuesday evening kids would pour into the church sanctuary and be entertained by great music (recorded and live) blaring over a state-of-the-art sound system, creative dramas and skits, highly competitive games, and a multimedia show, topped off with a challenging talk by the director.

A few of the elders began mumbling when they saw the bills; others questioned the wear and tear on the sanctuary (pews aren't built to have kids stand on them or to have relay races run through and over them). They were conflicted: Isn't this what they'd prayed for and dreamed about? But they wondered about the price (now adding up to thousands of dollars) and the toll the ministry was exacting on the church facilities.

That's the tension we all face, isn't it? To be crass—how much is a teenager worth? On the one hand, we can argue that every soul is priceless, so we should spend whatever it takes to reach young people these days. If a hi-tech youth lounge and programs with all the bells and whistles draws them in, then how could anyone possibly object?

But the counterargument talks about waste and using resources *wisely*, especially in light of some of the crying needs of the world. Does God really want our students stuffing their faces during a burger-eating contest, while teenagers living not that far away are scavenging garbage dumps looking for food?

Now, I'm as good at rationalizing as the next person. So I can remember several extravagant youth events that we sponsored at the time, and I could argue for their validity even to this day. After all, teenagers are used to first-class, quality entertainment, and the church should do nothing less than the best! Right?

But if I were to be completely honest, I'd have to say that my deeper motives were self-oriented—much of that time I was meeting my own needs. I enjoyed the spotlight and the attention and the great feeling that comes with large attendance.

So the first question we should ask ourselves is this: *Will this event, activity, or program really move us toward our ministry's goals?* For example, if the goal is evangelism, is this the most effective method for reaching unbelieving students? If the goal is discipleship (spiritual formation, Christian growth), will this get us there?

Other questions are also helpful:

- Will this enhance personal, relational ministry?
- What other options do we have?

Sometimes we repeat certain activities simply because that's the way we've always done things...or they were successful in the past...or the students liked them. Instead, we need to ask the hard questions and be willing to make a change if the answers aren't what they should be.

If we think it through and expand our options, we can often find ways to accomplish our goals with much less expense than we might think. The best way to do this is to pretend that we have virtually *no* youth ministry funds to use and our students have limited financial resources. (Note: In most churches around the world, this is a reality.)

Over the years I (Dave) have written hundreds of games and crowd-breakers (honest!), and I've used most of them. What I've found is that the inexpensive ones can be just as fun and effective as the expensive ones. Consider, for example, all of the variations of charades, relay races, and scavenger hunts that use only those props found on site. In a park or forest preserve, you can use grass, dirt, trees, dandelions, leaves, sticks, stones, litter or trash, insects, pine cones, and so on. At the beach you can use sand, of course—running, crawling, skipping, rolling, digging, building, or burying people in it—water, and the combination of the two. In a crowded room you can use improvised skits, word play, hand motions, leaning, and working with others. Young Life has pioneered and perfected singing as a powerful youth ministry tool (it just takes a guitar, a leader, and some songbooks).

I know youth directors who spend a fortune on props like water guns, finger rockets, exotic foods, prizes, and electronic toys. I'm sure the students love those games and contests, but probably not any more than they do the cheaper variety.

And what about retreats and trips? Sure, a ski trip to the Alps would certainly generate some excitement (and the chaperones would love it).

But if we really pay attention to our goals, then we'll probably discover that we could accomplish what we want much closer to home.

The point is not to do everything on the cheap, but to be wise in the use of our financial resources. Why spend money on something when we don't need to? And if we save money *here*, then we can spend it *there*—where we really need to.

In all this discussion of finances, spending, and resources, we need to remember that everything belongs to God: "The earth is the Lord's, and everything in it, the world, and all who live in it" (Psalm 24:1). This means that while God allows us to take care of and use a variety of resources, he's still the owner of them—they are his.

That's why the Bible talks so much about stewardship. Being a good steward means using and investing resources responsibly and wisely. This doesn't mean being so tight that we begrudge every dollar spent. People should be paid fairly (including youth ministers), and we should expect to pay for what we need and use. But we shouldn't waste those valuable resources or spend them foolishly.

More than the IRS or our supervisors, we answer to God—he's in charge.

Discussion Questions

1. What expensive props or other ministry resources (books, equipment, and so on) have you purchased or rented in the last six months? How might you have achieved the same results less expensively?

2. What expensive events, activities, trips, or retreats do you sponsor in a typical ministry year? What less-expensive options can you think of to get the same results?

For Further Study

• Spend some time reflecting on the great truth proclaimed in Psalm 24:1—that God owns *everything*. If it all belongs to him, then how should that alter the way we handle and spend the church's finances?

• Read the short account in Luke 21:1-4 about the poor widow who put her two small copper coins into the temple treasury. Think about the lower-income families in your church who sacrifice to give to the church. Ask yourself this: *In the last month, have I used church funds to do frivolous, unnecessary things with the hard-earned money that the church members have given?*

Avoiding an Avoidable Mess

• Be creative. Think outside the box. Whenever possible, make it your goal to do more with less.

• Model stewardship for your staff and students.

HELPING STUDENTS' FAMILIES STRETCH THEIR DOLLARS

One criticism of many church groups and youth organizations is that their activities cost too much and thereby exclude many students. The perception is that some youth ministries are like a country club, and only those who can afford the costs of membership need apply.

Many of the youth leaders we interviewed for this book expressed regret for unintentionally excluding students because of money. When my (Dave) daughters were in middle school and high school and active in our church's youth ministry, I remember feeling the bite of the activities' expenses (retreat, mission trip, ski trip, concert, big event, and so forth). I wondered how some families in the church could afford to keep sending their kids. It's not that the youth director was being irresponsible or extravagant—everything just seemed to cost a lot. And as a parent, I could feel the pinch.

So how can we provide quality programs without excluding those with limited resources? Here are some principles and suggestions:

Help Them on the Income Side

Most church youth groups sponsor fund-raisers of one sort or another: Car washes, work-a-thons, other-thons, gift-wrap services, candy sales, dinners, special programs, garage or rummage sales, babysitting, and many other creative options.

Before announcing a fund-raising event, check with your supervisor to make sure it doesn't conflict with any written—or unwritten—policies or the calendar of events (especially important in a church). In most churches, for example, a "Las Vegas Night" of gambling probably won't go over too well.

You should also make sure your fund-raising event is really worth the effort—especially if the main goal is to raise a large sum. Groups can expend tons of effort to host an event, only to raise a few dollars per student. Unless the primary goal is something else (like fun or fellowship), such events may not be the best use of your time.

Here's an important consideration that's often overlooked: Be sure to communicate the purpose of each fund-raising activity and how the money will be distributed. Some groups raise funds for a specific trip (like a mission trip) and then lower the cost of the trip for *everyone* who's going. That's okay—but it might be preferable to put the money into an account that can provide scholarships to help lower the costs for those who really need it.

Respect Their Dignity

Instead of offering a free ride to students who need economic assistance, provide ways for these students to earn their way. It's a well-documented fact that while a handout may help a needy person immediately, it can also harm the person long term, as he may become dependant on the handouts. And most people, especially adolescents, don't want to be known as charity cases.

Instead of a gift or grant, you can give needy students opportunities to gather the necessary funds for the event or trip. Here are a few ways:

- Scholarships: Let everyone know that scholarships are available and then work out a reasonable application process.
- Work: Allow individuals to earn their way by doing work for you, around the church, or for other benefactors.
- Matching funds: Set aside some of the fund-raising proceeds for a "matching fund." Then use this money to match what kids raise through other fund-raising efforts during a certain time period (usually those who need the money most will take advantage of this opportunity).
- Loan: Be quick to offer to lend money to students who can't pay for the trip or activity right then but probably will be able to pay later.

You can announce these opportunities to your group and see who responds. But you should also take the initiative to approach, individually and privately, those students whom you know could use the help. You could say something like this: "Hey, I know things have been tough lately with your dad losing his job and all. Let's work on getting you one of those scholarships," or something similar.

Work behind the scenes by talking about the situation with a student's parents. You may even want to work out a way to give the parents some money that they, in turn, can give to the son or daughter to pay for the event. (Or they could give the trip as a birthday or Christmas gift.) In many churches the deacons maintain a fund to help needy families, so this might be an option as well.

Create Teachable Moments

Paying for ministry activities, especially big-ticket ones, can provide a great opportunity for teaching lessons on stewardship, budgeting, and other aspects of financial planning. When I (Dave) led the YFC chapter in the New Orleans area several years ago, a very creative Campus Life staff member, Shane O'Hara, designed a simple but ingenious way to help kids financially.

Most of Shane's students came from middle- or lower-income working families—so they didn't have lots of discretionary funds. And every Christmas vacation, we'd join other southern chapters of YFC in Gatlinburg, Tennessee, for "Winter Holiday." The trip's cost wasn't exorbitant, but it was still a bit pricey for many. So Shane opened a special bank account and worked with kids to establish their own individual accounts and make regular contributions to save up for the trip (much like banks used to do with "Christmas Clubs"). Shane asked a volunteer to manage the funds and give regular reports to the savers.

Did it work? One year he had more than 100 students from one high school go to Gatlinburg with us. In addition to paying for the trip themselves, those teenagers also learned the discipline of saving.

You can probably think of some other ways to turn this financial challenge into a teaching opportunity.

Remember That Investment Means Commitment

Some youth ministries seek to make all their activities free to students by putting all expenses for every event into the larger church budget. This way, the reasoning goes, finances will never be a barrier to participation. Others explain this by noting that the church seems to always be asking for money, so why nickel-and-dime the members to death with these other little things?

Those points seem valid, except for one small problem: People tend to be less committed when they've made no investment—when nothing is at stake. A parenting seminar that costs $10 a person or $15 a couple is usually better attended than a free one, despite the number of people who sign up ahead of time. People who pay $7 for a book used in an adult Sunday school class are more likely to show up and get involved. Those who make a nonrefundable deposit are much more likely to go on the trip.

Certainly most facets of the ministry should have no charge. Sunday school classes, youth group meetings, light refreshments, small groups, counseling, the occasional youth group party, and similar services and programs should all be free. But with special events like a youth group banquet, a concert, or a special trip, you should charge a nominal fee since not only do people expect to pay for these things, but also the financial investment increases their commitment. However, the cost of full involvement in ministry events should be within reach of every student.

Discussion Questions

1. What would you guess is the average annual income for the families of your students?

2. What students in your group seem to struggle financially?

3. What can you do to help students and their parents afford to partici-pate in the ministry?

For Further Study

• Spend some time reflecting on Matthew 25:31-40. In your group who are "the least of these"?

• Meditate on James 2:2-9. When have you been guilty of favoring "rich" over "poor" in your ministry?

Avoiding an Avoidable Mess

• With your staff discuss and identify some possible financial barriers to student participation in the ministry.

• Design a strategy for the income side of the ministry, including fund-raising events, work opportunities, scholarships, and financial counseling.

MAINTAINING FINANCIAL INTEGRITY

As structured as I (Len) am now—with all my fanatical list making and the obsessive-compulsive tendencies that drive my family nuts—it's hard to believe I was once a carefree youth director.

Nevertheless, it's true. I was Mr. Casual. Mr. Laidback. I flew by the proverbial seat of my pants (usually short pants). With my wrinkled untucked shirts, flip-flops, cool Wilson gym bag (instead of a fuddy-duddy briefcase), and my assorted index cards containing my scribbled notes (instead of a big fat Day-Timer—God forbid!), my whole life screamed, "Whatever!" And I puzzled over why some parents didn't take me seriously.

This chronic sloppiness and disorganization extended to my finances, too. Balance my checkbook? Are you *kidding* me? Whenever the bank statements got too overwhelming, I simply closed the old account and opened a new one.

I followed the same loosey-goosey approach when it came to professional expenses. Our church wasn't exactly Ernst & Young when it came to accounting, but I was asked to keep track of my mileage (that is, miles driven for ministry-related business). At the end of each month, I was expected to add up the miles and submit a form in order to receive a reimbursement. Fairly clear and painless, right?

Nah. I tried this system for a while, but it involved *way* too many steps, procedures, and items to keep up with. Eventually I resorted to handing our sweet bookkeeper my Shell credit card receipts (whatever ones I could find, that is). Then a few days later, she'd hand me a check.

I suppose I reasoned, "*Most* of my driving involves running kids around, or going to their games and other activities. And the driving that's *not* directly related to *youth events*—well, it's still related to the *youth director*. And, anyway, it's not like we're talking about a lot of money." (In those days I could fill up my little Toyota for about $12 and drive 300 or 400 miles!)

I remember feeling a faint twinge of conscience the first few times I did this, but nobody ever said anything. And you'd be surprised (or maybe you wouldn't) at how quickly you can learn to ignore the nudges of God's Spirit.

Five or six years later—after seminary, now living four states away and volunteering with the youth group at another church—the memory of all this came flooding back. Suddenly, I was stricken with guilt. A disturbing, unrelenting guilt. And the truth hit me: I *felt* guilty because I *was* guilty. I was a seminary-educated thief! I'd stolen from my church! For a couple of days, I tried to evade this heavy sense of conviction. But it wouldn't go away. God wasn't going to let me off the hook. Not this time.

So finally I did the only thing I knew to do: I wrote a letter of explanation and confession to my former pastor or boss. I did a bit of calculating, and then I enclosed a check to the church for $500—which was a whopping sum of money for me then (and now!).

Is it a pain to follow financial guidelines and keep accurate records? Sure. But it's nothing like the pain of easily avoidable failure and regret. Integrity costs a lot. But it's not nearly as expensive as guilt.

Discussion Questions

1. With regard to personal finances, how would you describe your habits?

2. Have you ever been in trouble financially? When? What happened?

3. What are the practical benefits of being an absolute stickler to financial rules and regulations?

For Further Study

• Spend some time reflecting on Psalm 32:1-5. How does David describe the period of time in which he resisted God's conviction?

• Ponder Proverbs 10:9 and the importance of integrity.

Avoiding an Avoidable Mess

• If your church or ministry doesn't have a handbook containing policies about the handling of finances, then make an appointment with your supervisor and ask, "What are the rules?"

• Get the name of a respected accountant (maybe someone in your congregation). Invite her to lunch. Bring a notepad. Ask this expert to give you a crash course in what to do and what not do, wise practices and no-nos.

LIVING ON A YOUTH WORKER'S SALARY

If you're a volunteer, then you can skip this section. Go have a latte and send the bill to Youth Specialties. (Just kidding, YS!) But if a job in youth ministry is your way to pay the bills, then keep reading...

Unless you're employed by a wealthy church or an organization with money to burn, your beginning salary as a youth worker probably won't nudge you into the upper middle class. In fact, youth pastors are often the lowest-paid staff members in a church.

That doesn't mean you shouldn't be paid a decent salary. But you may feel like it's a struggle to make ends meet on your take-home pay, especially when you're just starting out. And you may also feel frustrated, at times, if you can't afford to live in your ministry area or buy the same clothes or "toys" your students enjoy.

Then you go to your high school or college reunion and you feel better, right? Wrong! Not when you hear glowing reports of a classmate on the corporate fast track, a former roommate who made a killing in the stock market, and a friend who just finished medical school. They seem to be set for life—no financial worries—while you live from paycheck to paycheck.

But you knew all this before you signed up. You chose youth ministry because God called you and because you love teenagers. You're not in this for the money. If status, possessions, and walk-around cash were high on your list of priorities, you would have taken a different career path.

Learning to live on the average youth worker's salary can stretch one's faith. My (Dave) brother, Paul, worked in Campus Life, just as I did. When I asked him to contribute a story for this section, he shared the following.

My wife, Darian, and I learned our most valuable lessons in finances when we had the least amount of income. Structuring costs for food, energy, home expenses, and entertainment were a necessity, especially when you worked for a parachurch youth ministry. Not only did the ministry not pay a great deal, but we also had to raise our support. Thus, we had to know how every penny was spent because we didn't know if we'd receive the next paycheck on time, if at all.

But sometimes good planning isn't enough. Sometimes there appears to be no good financial solution. So you do your best and pray that God will make up the difference.

When Darian was pregnant with our first two children (twins), we were faced with some serious financial issues. We would lose her salary (25 percent more than mine) and double our dependents, meaning more money for food, clothing, diapers, medicine, and so on. Besides that, we had the extra hospital costs for the delivery and care of twins over and above our insurance coverage. And in addition to that, I was taking graduate courses. Financially speaking, this was like an earthen dam trying to hold back the hurricane floodwaters of debt. The outlook wasn't encouraging, and something was bound to give way.

To make matters worse, the delivery of the twins had some complications. Our son needed to be on a respirator because of premature lung development, and Darian needed more surgery because of post-delivery hemorrhaging. Our whole extended family was concerned and in prayer for us. Thankfully, God pulled us through the physical issues, but what about the bills?

During this time our organization changed health insurance carriers, and we were told that our old carrier would cover the delivery costs, since the pregnancy happened during its tenure. They wouldn't cover the costs associated with the resulting complications, however. What happened next was miraculous to us! We learned that the new health insurance policy wouldn't cover the delivery, but it would cover the complications. Thus, we had the benefit of both policies, and our hospital costs were nothing.

Just as miraculous was God's provision to pay for graduate school. I've never considered myself a rocket scientist, but I applied for a few scholarships and got them. Combining those scholarships with our education policy, my out-of-pocket costs for graduate school totaled nothing!

These events all happened more than 40 years ago, but we'll always remember them. God provided for us, completely.

It's amazing when we look back and see how God provided for our needs! But that doesn't mean we'll never be required to stretch our resources or make financial sacrifices.

Again, we must emphasize that churches and Christian organizations shouldn't expect their employees to live at subsistence or poverty level. No one, especially those with youthful idealism and energy, should be taken advantage of and *used*. Yet even in the most generous institutions, youth workers won't be paid very much. "Not-for-profit" means just that—most Christian ministries can't fill their coffers by selling products; they exist through the donations of those who believe in the cause.

So you'd better get used to living on less. But this doesn't have to be a terrible experience. In fact, you can see it as an adventure, a challenge. Looking back on their lives together, many married couples will say that their best years were when they had to struggle to make ends meet. So your initial years in ministry are an important time to learn how to manage money and wisely use the resources you *do* have.

This begins with a personal budget. If you need help with this, then find a financial planner in your church to help you put (and keep) your personal finances in order. Be sure to include a savings plan, even if you put aside only a small amount each month. Ask this person to hold you accountable, too, so you'll live within this budget.

Make sure you have good health insurance—most Christian ministries understand this need and include it in the benefits package. And work with the leaders to add a retirement plan to their personnel policy.

Here's a caution: Remember that money can't buy happiness. We tell that to our students, of course. But we can fall for the lie ourselves as we watch a steady stream of ads espousing the "good life" of affluence. So as you work hard at stretching that paycheck, remember that an older car can provide transportation just as effectively as a new one; nutritious and tasty meals don't have to be exotic; entertainment doesn't have to be expensive; and it's the family that makes the home, not its furnishings.

Discussion Questions

1. On a scale of 1 to 10, with 1 being impoverished and 10 being rich, where would you put your present financial situation? If you're on or near the bottom of that scale, what factors put you there? What keeps you there?

2. Who do you know that might be willing to help you design and stick to a budget?

3. What steps can you take to make your income go farther?

For Further Study

• Spend some time reflecting on Luke 3:14, where John the Baptist tells some repentant soldiers what they should do: "Don't extort money and don't accuse people falsely—be content with your pay."

• Meditate on the following verses: Philippians 4:12, 1 Timothy 6:6, and Hebrews 13:5. Then finish this sentence: I have learned to be content...

Avoiding an Avoidable Mess

• Learn your church or organization's personnel policies, including sabbaticals, maternity or family leaves, study and book funds, mileage reimbursements, and so forth.

• Check out Crown Financial Ministries (www.Crown.org) and plan to attend a seminar near you.

• Consider how your personal stewardship teaches others who are watching you.

THE MORAL **MINEFIELD**

"Never be alone in a car with a girl," he said. And he was serious.
My ministry compatriots and I (Dave) were being briefed by Clayton
Baumann, my new boss in YFC. Fresh out of college, we'd been hired to
pioneer Campus Life in Chicago's northwest suburbs, and we thought
we knew what that would involve. Virtually every aspect of the ministry
would be built on relationships with students in the communities and
high schools to which we each had been assigned. That would mean
going on campus as often as possible, attending school and community
events, and just hanging out with individuals and groups. Certainly the
relationship-building efforts would include members of the opposite
sex, right?

As Clayton added other similar warnings and cautions, we pushed
back, questioning the policy and his reasoning. He explained about temptation, teenage crushes, and the "appearance of evil"—and we listened.
I'm not sure I agreed with the policy at the time, but I followed it.

Looking back, I'm glad I did!

Back then I was just 22 years old. I thought and felt as if I were a full
generation older than the high school students I'd be trying to reach.
Those three or four years of age difference seem like a huge gap to a
young twenty-something. But over the years, I've realized how small
that gap really is. I've also realized that Clayton's wise counsel probably
saved me and the ministry from a host of problems. Looking back, I
realize that I was working in a moral minefield.

That's what we'll be discussing in this chapter.

ABOVE REPROACH

During the first decade of the twenty-first century, allegations of clergy
sexual misconduct seemed to arise weekly. Although revelations about
the sexual abuse of children by some Catholic priests garnered the
most headlines, youth directors were included as well. Two particular
incidents stand out in my memory—both involving youth ministers in

prominent evangelical churches. But how many other youth leaders were quietly dismissed by other churches and Christian organizations, as teenagers and their parents were counseled privately and as threatened lawsuits were settled out of court?

Youth leaders should never have romantic relationships with the students they're working with. Never. We cannot overemphasize that point. Imagine the devastating impact on the adolescent psyche and the tremendous betrayal of trust from a sexual relationship between a leader and a teenager. Sexual impropriety must be avoided at all costs—because it is sin, because of the integrity of the ministry, and because of the effects. It will mess up the lives of the students, the life of the leader, and the ministry.

The spate of publicized incidents and allegations of sexual misconduct by clergy, coaches, teachers, and other authority figures have made people much more aware of and sensitive to the possibility of inappropriate behavior between adults and children. Allegations and accusations—even those which later prove to be false—can ruin ministries and lives. We live in a litigation-happy society—people want to sue over anything and everything. And all this can make youth leaders gun-shy, feeling as though they're assumed to be guilty until proven innocent.

Every person and every action is scrutinized. But whining about it doesn't help—that's just the way of the world these days. So if we want to continue working with kids, then we'll have to be careful and live, as much as possible, above reproach.

No one's perfect—we all make mistakes and miscues. But part of our job as youth leaders is to be positive and godly role models for our students. We should take seriously the biblical principle of caring for the weaker brother or sister (Romans 14:1-15:3, 1 Corinthians 10:23-

If your church or group doesn't have a policy on sexual misconduct, write one—for yourself and for all the other paid and volunteer staff members. That's a place to start.

When working with college men one summer, I discovered that most of them were struggling with pornography. That fall I met with our new youth pastor—my wife and I were volunteer youth leaders at our church. He was single and popular and had an open-door policy with students dropping by his house all the time. I shared with him my concern about the pornography problem, with Christians having and using easy access to Internet porn. I encouraged him to live beyond reproach, and I asked what measures he had in place to limit his personal access to porn. He said he didn't agree that such preventive measures were necessary. He asserted, in fact, that he needed to have access so he could learn to say "no" in the midst of temptation.

My mind flashed back to the dozens of college students I'd talked with about their habits and my great concern for the future leadership of our church—including future husbands—and those who might be influenced by such thinking. So obviously I was a bit sensitive to the subject, and I may have come on a little strong. But that day I gave the youth pastor a choice. I told him he needed to get a filter that would work on his home computer, or my wife and I would stop working with the ministry. I also said I felt so strongly about this issue that I'd probably go to the church leaders and ask for his immediate dismissal if he refused.

The young man was shocked by my response, but he promised to put such a filter in place. I don't know if he did or not. But over the following months, his philosophy started to show up in the movies the students saw sitting on the shelves at his house, as well as in his arrogance toward the people in leadership. Soon parents began limiting the access this youth pastor could have to their children. And eventually he was fired.

The point I was trying to make with this youth pastor—which he chose to ignore—is that we need to live in such a way that everything we do can be imitated by those who follow us, with the goal being that they will be more Christlike for having followed us.

—*Dave Wager*

33). Although we are free, as mature adults and Christians, to indulge in certain behaviors (entertainment options, alcohol consumption, conversation topics, and so on), we should refrain from flaunting our freedom and, in the process, cause a weaker, younger, and immature believer to stumble in his faith.

Setting a good example includes how we dress and speak. Our clothing shouldn't be sexually suggestive or overly revealing (that includes swimming attire!). And we should avoid crude, sexist, or suggestive talk (double meanings, too), steering clear of bathroom humor in comments, jokes, skits, games, and other aspects of the ministry. Hopefully, we'll be able to say as Paul did, "Follow my example, as I follow the example of Christ" (1 Corinthians 11:1). That's not being phony; it's being sensitive...and responsible.

In How We Relate to the Opposite Sex

Some youth workers are mighty chummy, almost flirtatious, with certain students. That can happen for several reasons: The youth worker may, in fact, be sexually attracted to a teenager in the group; the youth worker may simply have a very friendly and outgoing personality; the student may use flirtatious behavior to get the youth worker's attention, and the youth worker responds; and so forth. Regardless of the reason, we need to be extremely careful in this regard. We certainly don't want other students or parents to make the wrong assumptions.

I (Dave) once confronted a guy on our staff about his habit of surrounding himself with adoring females. He assured me he was just fooling around—nothing was going on. And when I said that others might get the wrong idea, he replied, "That's *their* problem, not mine!" But, in fact, *their* problem can become *ours* very quickly.

These guidelines can help youth workers avoid situations that can lead to inappropriate behavior, as well as the appearance of inappropriate behavior.[4]

- Never be alone in a car with a member of the opposite sex. (Clayton was right.) If a student needs a ride to or from church, solicit an adult leader of the same sex to pick up that student or take other students along with you for the ride. Train your volunteers not to leave you alone with a student of the opposite sex.
- When counseling a student of the opposite sex, do so in a public place, such as the school cafeteria, school hallways, in an office or other room with the door standing open and other adults in the vicinity, or in the student's home *with the parents nearby.*
- Share your standards with others who can help. Make sure other office staff members are aware of the times when you're counseling the opposite sex. If your office door doesn't have a window, maintain an open-door policy or insist that a spouse or other adult leader be involved in conversations that are too confidential for the door to remain open. If a student demands to meet with you privately and without anyone else's knowledge, then be cautious and prayerfully consider not meeting with the student.
- Hold your adult volunteers to the same standards. Ministry can just as easily be affected by the missteps of an adult volunteer. Train your compatriots on the importance of maintaining boundaries with students of the opposite sex.
- Speaking of counseling, don't counsel anyone late into the night during a retreat, camp, or similar setting. Nothing very positive happens after 11 p.m.
- Don't *initiate* physical contact—especially frontal hugs—with a young person of the opposite sex.

Charise was a very attractive, sweet, funny teen who had a crush on me, I think. (I was probably 23; she was a mature 17?) And one night at a conference, after all the sessions had ended, we stayed up *very* late in the cafeteria or big meeting room just talking. We were communicating and connecting at a pretty honest, vulnerable level, when suddenly we realized we were all alone, and it was dark, and we *both* were confronted by a powerful physical attraction.

We didn't *do* anything (thank God!!), but it was a case of two God-loving (yet hormone-filled) young adults finding themselves in an intoxicating, confusing situation. Had I been a 28-year-old grad student and she a 22-year-old college senior, who knows? Maybe a date wouldn't have raised any eyebrows. But I was a youth pastor, and she was one of my students.

I just remember how intense it all felt—the chemistry, electricity, and so on. Yikes! It's scary how close to the edge we really were.

—*Name Withheld*

4. Special thanks to Jeff Dye for contributing several of these guidelines.

- Don't indulge in sex talk (jokes, discussions of certain TV shows or movies, and so on).
- On long bus or van rides, don't sit with a member of the opposite sex—especially if sleeping is involved.

In short, stay out of compromising situations. These guidelines aren't difficult to follow—they just take sensitivity and planning.

Building relationships with students is critical to youth ministry. We must make sure, however, that our interactions with students are healthy, appropriate, and above reproach. A simple accusation of inappropriate behavior can cause great damage to one's ministry, marriage, family, and reputation. Our responsibility is to enforce standards that will keep and protect us from compromising situations.

In How We Handle Money

Another common accusation against the church relates to finances. Unfortunately, this has some justification, since a number of stories of misappropriation of church funds have hit the news. As we saw in chapter 9, we need to be careful how we handle money—since we may sometimes be trusted to handle very large sums of it. And just as with sexual temptation, we need to realize that money can be very alluring, especially when finances are tight. So here are some guidelines for being above reproach in this sensitive area:

- Bring all funds into the church or organization's financial system. Work out a system that works well for you and for the financial secretary.
- Keep funds safe, perhaps even depositing them yourself and as soon as possible into the appropriate account.
- Don't allow students or parents to write checks to *you* for a ministry event or purchase. If you're concerned that someone might try to claim a tax deduction for their camp fee, then you could ask them to make out the check to the name of your organization and put the words CAMP FEE on the memo line.
- Keep accurate records of who's paid and who still owes money for any event or activity with a charge. Some kids will be caught by surprise and will want to pay the fee later. That's all right, but be sure to let them know that you'll remind them of their debt.
- Don't misuse your tax-exempt status to purchase personal items.

The pull of the "love of money" (1 Timothy 6:10) doesn't stop at the church door. Be careful. And let your students and their parents know that you operate under specific financial policies and aren't fooling around with the funds.

Discussion Questions

1. In your adolescent years, who provided a good example of what an adult Christian should be? What can you do to model Christian values to others?

2. What changes should you make in your personal life to safeguard against causing a "weaker" believer to stumble?

3. When might you find yourself in an awkward situation with a member of the opposite sex? What can you do to avoid situations like that?

4. What controls or accountability systems do you have for handling money?

5. What changes should you make to be more responsible in that area?

For Further Study

• Spend some time reflecting on Romans 14:1-15:3 and 1 Corinthians 10:23-33. Which of your students would fall in the category of "weak faith"?

• Meditate on 1 Timothy 3:2 and 4:12. Consider how these passages relate to youth ministers living above reproach.

Avoiding an Avoidable Mess

• In consultation with your senior pastor (or director), decide on a staff "code of conduct" for these areas: Entertainment, personal habits, dating or marriage relationships, recreation, and so on. Then present the code to your staff, explaining your rationale.

• With your staff, talk through the guidelines for dealing with the opposite sex and handling money (as outlined above). Let them know that the goal is to be above reproach.

STUDENT-VOLUNTEER ATTRACTIONS

News flash—adolescents don't check their hormones at the door when they come to your group. And the same thing is true for youth workers—full time, part time, volunteer, single, or married. *All* are susceptible to lust and other temptations.

Unfortunately, the youth ministry battlefield is littered with fallen leaders—felled by self-inflicted wounds! All the more reason to insist on those opposite-sex guidelines for *all* staff members.

But we want to focus on volunteers here for a couple of reasons: Accountability and age. Let's take a quick look at each.

First, volunteers don't tend to have the same structures of accountability that surround most paid staff. Someone in a paid position is responsible to a supervisor. And hopefully the supervisor, through regular meetings and performance reviews, asks tough questions about ministry goals, plans, policies, and procedures. Plus, because a church staff person has visibility within the congregation, parents will know who to approach with their questions and concerns.

A volunteer, however, can fly under the radar and be difficult to detect. Many youth leaders recruit volunteers and then charge them with building relationships with students, leading a small group, helping with meetings, or some other aspect of the ministry. But who's making sure they're steering clear of the moral mines?

We need to build an accountability system into the ministry plan. This may mean having volunteers report their campus visits and what they did while they were there—who they met, when, and where. Volunteers need to know that we're interested in all their ministry activities, not just the events where we can see them.

The second issue is age. Many youth ministry volunteers are only a few years older than the young people with whom they're working. Many churches use high school students as volunteers in their junior high ministry. And college students often work with both early and middle adolescents. So the difference in ages between student and leader may be just a year or two—certainly within the dating range. At that age, with single young adults looking for romance and high school students dealing with hormones and sexual attraction, the combination can be deadly.

When that beautiful cheerleader or studly football player from the local university begins volunteering in the church youth ministry, you may feel great about the energy, charisma, and relationship-building skills they bring. You might even see a bump in group attendance and interest, and you'd definitely appreciate the positive role models that these young leaders would provide. But along with these benefits come potential opposite-sex issues that you'd be foolish to ignore.

That's why we need to make the wall between student and leader well defined and clear. We have to let young volunteers know that we expect them to adhere to specific guidelines and standards—no exceptions.

- Brock, college sophomore, likes the attention he receives at club from the kids, especially the girls. *He needs to be warned—he can be charming and nice but not flirtatious.*
- Kelly, college freshman, spent some time talking with Erik after the group Bible study. The next day they were text-messaging back and forth. *She needs to be careful and told to keep text-messaging with guy students to a minimum—and to avoid anything that might encourage romantic feelings.*
- Devon, college junior, feels strongly attracted to Emma, a high school senior. He'd like to ask her out. *He needs to be told that this is prohibited as long as he is on staff. In fact, to protect the ministry, he probably should wait at least six months after leaving the staff before pursuing Emma.*
- A few high school guys visit Michelle at her school and stop by her dorm room. *She needs to be careful she doesn't encourage any of the guys to visit her alone.*

Sometimes we create or heighten the problems by putting students and staff in compromising situations—students sitting on leaders' laps, games that feature close contact, frank sex discussions, talk of questionable TV shows and movies, and so forth. Inadvertently, we can be part of the problem.

The temptations *will* be there; that's normal whenever young men and women spend time together. So we need to be realists and remain wise. This means we must stop ministry-destroying incidents before they occur.

Discussion Questions

1. What benefits do you see from utilizing young-adult volunteers in your ministry? What potential limitations and drawbacks are there?

2. What can you do to help young staff members be positive role models for your students?

3. What policies and procedures can you put in place to prevent staff-student dating dilemmas and sexual disasters?

4. What ministry events or activities might involve the most temptation? What can you do to minimize those temptations?

For Further Study
• Spend some time reflecting on 2 Timothy 2:22. Consider what those "evil desires of youth" might be and how, exactly, to "flee" them.

• Meditate on Ephesians 4:25-32, Colossians 3:5, and Titus 2:6-8. Think about how these passages relate to working with volunteers in youth work.

Avoiding an Avoidable Mess
• Take a realistic view of human nature. Young people will be sexually attracted to one another; that's how God created us. Knowing that, take precautions and don't tempt fate.

• Tighten your screening process to help you enlist volunteers with the purest of motives.

• Meet individually with each ministry volunteer to go over ministry policies, procedures, and moral standards.

HUGS, BACK RUBS, AND OTHER SLIPPERY SLOPES
Let's face it: Some people are huggers. They like physical touch—it's their "love language." And through the years many studies have shown the value of human physical contact. Who hasn't appreciated a pat on the back, a high-five, or a hearty handshake? Touch can communicate warmth, affirmation, and belonging.

Certain kinds of touch also indicate solidarity and togetherness. We'll often see huge football players walk hand-in-hand to the center of the field for the coin toss. And we'll watch the celebration after a walk-off home run as the baseball players run to the pitcher's mound and hug and leap on each other after a big victory.

Perhaps the most powerful use of touch, however, is to express love. That's one reason a reassuring hug or a quick shoulder massage can easily turn into something a bit more meaningful—or at least it can be interpreted that way. The distance between a touch and a caress is pretty short.

Misinterpretation

Physical displays of affection can cause students to get the wrong idea, especially when the physical contact comes from someone they have feelings for. Consider these situations:

- Mike is a hugger—that's just his style. But occasionally he holds those hugs a bit too long. He also seems to enjoy hugging the attractive girls more often than the others.
- Candice's "love language" is touch, so she seems to put a hand on the arm or shoulder of everyone she talks to.
- Every time Thomas, the hot college volunteer, comes to a youth group meeting, a gaggle of younger girls rush to greet him with smiles and hugs—and he readily obliges.
- Katie is a massage therapist, so she'll often give quick, stress-relieving back rubs to those who want them. A couple of guys on the high school basketball team are always first in line.

We can't control what others think—some people will tend to get the wrong idea and misinterpret our actions no matter how careful we are. But that doesn't excuse sloppy or careless behavior. Why place ourselves and the youth ministry in jeopardy?

Because of the power of touch and the strong possibility of physical contact being misinterpreted, the best course of action would be to err on the conservative side. Does that mean hugs are verboten? No, but we need to approach them with care.

A good rule: *Don't initiate* the physical contact with the opposite sex. In other words, we

These days, most ministry employers are very cautious to avoid hiring the pedophile or the predator who'd become involved in ministry to fulfill his perverted desires. I've found the greater risk is identifying the ignorant, the prideful, the arrogant, and the needy people who allow their compassion to turn into a passion.

I count myself in the first group: *Ignorant* of what can happen in a ministry setting when someone looks up to you with almost worshipful admiration.

On the other side of the coin are the *prideful*—such as the former big man on campus who has graduated into the bigger world and now misses the attention he received in his younger days. I knew one staff person who always had the best-looking college girls for volunteers, but he struggled to find any guys to help him in his ministry. Hmmm…?

Then there's the *arrogant*—those who believe it couldn't happen to them because they are (choose one or more):

- Spiritual
- Mature

- Above it all
- Clad in the armor
- Angry at those who have similarly fallen

These types often fall the furthest and the hardest.

The *needy* don't always fall, but they're rarely in ministry for the right reasons. And they're highly susceptible to moral failure. Now, all of us are needy, but I'm talking about those people who never come to grips with their needs. They may believe no one notices their deep-rooted hurts, their anger, their desire to be liked, and so on. But it's so apparent to those around them that it seems almost unbeliev-able that they consider themselves equipped to minister to others.

—*Greg Monaco*

shouldn't run toward a student with our arms spread wide, inviting the person to be enfolded in our embrace. If a student decides to hug us—fine. We should hug that person back—not just stand there all limp. But we also shouldn't linger. If possible, make it a side hug.

At those times when physical touch is definitely needed and appropriate—to console, affirm, or encourage a person—be careful. In this area, especially, we need to be "as shrewd as snakes and as innocent as doves" (Matthew 10:16).

Discussion Questions

1. What ministry situations might encourage inappropriate physical contact?

2. Which students in your ministry are "huggers"? Which of your staff members fall into that category? Where might you fall on a hugging continuum?

3. When have you witnessed inappropriate physical touch in your ministry? What steps can you take to prevent that from happening in the future?

For Further Study

• Read *The Heart of the Five Love Languages* by Gary Chapman (Northfield, 2008) to get an understanding of how people communicate love to each other. (This book was also referenced in chapter 3.) See if you can determine the dominant "love language" for yourself and others in the ministry.

• Check out *The Power of Touch: The Basis for Survival, Health, Intimacy, and Emotional Well-Being* (Hay House, 1999) by Phyllis Davis, Ph.D. or a similar secular counseling book.

Avoiding an Avoidable Mess

• Have a thorough discussion of this topic with your staff members.

• Agree on guidelines for hugs and other appropriate physical touch.

COMPUTERS AND THE INTERNET

Technological advances and the digital revolution have changed the world dramatically in the past decade—and more changes are sure to come. Consider how such advances have impacted society in general: Music stores, newspapers, and traditional bookstores are all in trouble; politicians raise untold millions through the Internet; Facebook and other social networks are booming; and online news outlets spread word of world events almost instantaneously.

Many newer technologies have been a tremendous boon to youth ministry. Leaders can communicate with students almost instantaneously through text-messaging and cell phones. Creative Web sites can draw in visitors and communicate with the faithful. And consider all of the ministry resources available online: Video clips on YouTube and GodTube, Bible study tools, and downloadable curricula (just to name a few). Even games and other meeting activities have benefited. Not long ago, youth leaders worked hard to get enough Polaroid cameras for a scavenger hunt activity; now digital cameras are everywhere. Before, leaders had to spend several hours putting together a creative slide show; now we can create that show in minutes on the computer.

But technology has also brought ministry challenges, especially when we consider the moral minefield. These days porn is available at every turn, sexual predators troll MySpace and other social networks, and hucksters of all varieties pursue potential customers through spam and other means.

Technology has made every ministry event public. These days, just about everyone has easy access to a digital camera (think cell phone) and the ability to transport those images almost anywhere. Not long ago, memories of a camp or retreat would be confined to word-of-mouth retelling or, at least, waiting until the photos were developed. Late-night discussions in the cabin were relatively private, and pranks and embarrassing moments were witnessed by only a few. But recording events and interactions has become incredibly easy—and doesn't always result in positive outcomes.

Consider the case of Tony, a college-aged youth ministry volunteer who started texting with some students, emailing back and forth with them, and even going camping and hiking with some of the high school guys in his small group. They'd talk pretty candidly about sex stuff (normal teenage questions and other issues). On one camping trip, they all skinny-dipped; and somebody took a few digital pictures (just rearview shots). The JPEGs got posted on the Internet, and a mom found out. The next thing you know, the authorities seized this young man's computer and found these sexually frank discussions. Now Tony was under arrest for indecent behavior with a juvenile and sentenced to 12 months in jail. Whether guilty or not (probably not), Tony was convicted by technology.

Tony's problem could have been avoided at several points. In every ministry situation or event, we need to ask ourselves what the reaction would be if that particular event were made public. We should encourage our staff members and volunteers to exercise great care in what they write via email or text message, recognizing that anything written in these forums can easily become public.

We also need to make sure all staff members steer clear of bad Internet habits. Encourage your staff to set good examples—in behavior, stewardship of time, thought life, and values.

When it comes to our students, we must understand the pervasive and persuasive influence of the Internet. We need to help students avoid porn and resist other media-driven temptations. (We can guide parents in this area as well.) We should also make our students aware of the dangers of many online networking sites, encouraging them not to reveal personal information and to look out for predators.

While using technology in the ministry, including text-messaging, we should help students build real, face-to-face relationships, to live in real community. If we aren't careful, our technological devices can isolate us from others. The youth ministry should be the ideal place to bring people together to make safe and Christ-centered connections.

Modern technology is amazing, and we should embrace it rather than fear it. But we also need to be aware of the dangers it poses and plan accordingly.

Discussion Questions

1. At what times have you been tempted by what's available on the Internet?

2. How have you kept yourself from those temptations?

3. How often do you use MySpace, Facebook, or a similar social networking site?

4. What ministry resources have you found on the Internet?

5. Describe a time when you and your ministry were vulnerable to experiencing something similar to what happened to Tony?

For Further Study
• Get copies of *Logged On and Tuned Out: A Non-Techie's Guide to Parenting a Tech-Savvy Generation* by Vicki Courtney (B&H Publishing Group, 2007). Read and discuss the book as a staff.

Avoiding an Avoidable Mess
• In a staff meeting, discuss the pros and cons of the Internet. Brainstorm ways to help educate students about how to use this tool in a responsible and God-honoring way.

• In planning your ministry activities and events, always ask this question: *What would happen if the community saw (or heard) this?* If you envision a bad potential outcome, change the activity or make sure no recording devices are present.

SAFETY ISSUES

Making safety the topic of chapter 11 is providential because nothing can bankrupt your ministry quicker than a safety issue—personal negligence leading to an injury or worse. Yet safety may be the most frequently overlooked or ignored aspect of the ministry, especially among new youth workers.

That's because they're young...and idealistic.

We know teenagers think and act as though they're invincible and immortal. They make dangerous choices and take foolish risks, just assuming everything will be okay. But we know better. And reality hits whenever we see the adolescent STD rates, hear stories of binge drinking and drug abuse, or read headlines about another fatal, late-night automobile accident.

Although we shake our heads and wish teenagers wouldn't act that way, most youth workers begin their ministries at an age that's not very far removed from those years, and thus they can have a similar tendency to make risky choices.

Idealism plays a role, too. Because as youth *ministers*, doing God's work and praying for God's protection, we may assume everything will turn out fine—even when we act impulsively or foolishly.

Just a year or so out of college, I (Dave) organized a trip from the Chicago suburbs to the Michigan dunes—about a two-and-a-half-hour drive and mostly on crowded tollways. We took three packed cars, and students drove two of them. On the way home, one of Chicago's finest pulled over one of my drivers. He'd apparently been driving barefoot, with his left foot somehow sticking out of the window. Later, I noticed the tires on his car were almost bald. Fortunately, all he got was a ticket.

Question: Why did I organize, authorize, and lead such an unsafe venture? Answer: Everyone was gung-ho about getting to the beach, and I was trying to build relationships with those guys. Safety issues didn't cross my mind.

They should have.

If I knew then what I know now, I would have been much more careful.

Hey, you're thinking, *someone ought to write a book about that!*

They have. Jack Crabtree has written the definitive book on youth ministry safety called *Better Safe Than Sued: Keeping Your Students and Ministry Alive* (Zondervan/Youth Specialties, 2008). And rather than rewrite or repeat that book here, we simply recommend it to you.

Thus, in the rest of this chapter, we'll be highlighting just a few important issues in ministry safety.

ADVANCED TROUBLESHOOTING AND CONTINGENCY PLANNING

"I didn't think the gun was loaded!"

"I assumed he was turning left."

"I thought the water was deeper."

Assumptions can kill. And when we have the safety responsibility for many young lives, we dare not make the wrong assumptions. Thinking through possible issues and problems in advance is vital.

Matt Tucker highlights this reality from his experience:

I've been a full-time youth minister since 1995. And over that span of time, much has changed in how I view the safety of my students. When I was just starting out, I put "being cool" above being responsible in many areas. This led me to allow certain activities to go on during retreats, trips, and special events that I never would allow now. In fact, if it weren't for God's protection, things could have been really bad. Fortunately, for the students' sake and my own, I had only a few kids get bumps and bruises during those early years. And one lesson I learned is not to *assume* people who should know better really do.

You've probably heard the quip that comes from the word assume. (When you *assume,* you make an *ass* out of *u* and *me.*) Well, that described me.

On one particular spring break trip, we were camping at a Christian campground in Florida. The camp director, who I *assumed* was safety conscious, offered to take our group tubing and skiing out on a lake with the camp's speedboat. I thought this was a fine idea, so the next day we packed up two vans full of students eager to have a good time.

The first group that went out on the lake consisted of two girls, two guys, and me. I was the video camera guy, and I thought I'd get some great footage of students skiing and tubing.

The two girls got on the tube first, and they were having a great time when I noticed several what I thought were logs floating in the middle of

Safety precautions will feel tedious and unnecessary. You'll want to take shortcuts. Being meticulous about permission slips is a drag. Creating bus rosters makes you feel like a Gestapo general —and if you don't already feel this way, then your students will make you! Volunteer applications and thorough screening seem so time-consuming when you desperately need workers. Risky games are fun. So you'll have to do what doesn't come naturally. You'll have to decide that the tedium, the red tape, the process, and the caution are worth it.

At the risk of sounding like an old, finger-wagging geezer, I'll say the blunt and painfully obvious truth (with a touch of drama thrown in): You'll think safety issues are only for other youth workers until a lawsuit is served or a death happens.

—Mark Oestreicher

the lake. Upon further observation, I noticed the "logs" were *moving*. My first instinct, since we were in Florida, was that they were actually alligators. But I quickly dismissed that thought because, again, I *assumed* our safety-conscious campground director knew something I didn't.

As soon as that thought passed through my brain, the girls fell off the tube, and the camp director whipped the boat around rather quickly to pick them up. I'll never forget his comment as he turned the wheel and looked back at the girls in the water: "Yeah, we'd better hurry. The gators are in the rut." I later learned that "in the rut" is a phrase used to describe alligators in mating season (when they're more aggressive).

When we picked up the girls, their eyes were three times their normal size, and they said, "Did you know there are alligators in the lake, and they were swimming toward us?"

Guess who heard about our little incident first? Yes, that's right, the parents. Fortunately, I had forgiving parents. But I learned a valuable lesson in "assuming." I now ask more questions, do a little research, and avoid the "assumption dilemma," as I like to call it.

Certainly we can't know everything about every ministry situation, so we don't know all the questions to ask. (For instance, who would have thought to ask about alligators?) But Matt makes a great point: We need to be careful about making any assumptions regarding safety.

Anticipating potential problems is equally important. Murphy's Law is real: If anything can go wrong, it will. And some say that Murphy was an optimist. So we need to think, in advance, about what could go wrong in any youth ministry event. This will help us prepare for something that might threaten our safety. In some cases, we'll avoid disaster.

At camp one summer, a new staff member had a great idea for a crowdbreaker—a peanut butter sandwich eating contest. Sounds innocent and harmless, right? Well, first he spread the peanut butter about half-an-inch thick on each slice of bread. Then he handed the sandwiches to the competitors and yelled, "Eat!" After a couple of bites, one student began to choke. The heavy layer of peanut butter had clogged his airway. Quick thinking by another counselor—who reached into the boy's mouth with two fingers and pulled out as much peanut butter as possible—saved the day and, possibly, a life.

Besides considering the potential for any nut allergies, the camp counselors should have anticipated the choking issue—a real possibility with any eating contest.

So think through what might go wrong during games, especially those that involve ingesting, falling, climbing, throwing, running, and extreme physical exertion. Even Olympic gymnasts use spotters, just in case they need help.

Imagining possible "what if" scenarios can also help us prepare to make midcourse adjustments and corrections, without sacrificing safety. We need to consider what might happen and make contingency plans. What if…

- We have car (van, bus) trouble?
- The weather turns nasty?
- Someone gets sick?
- A student has an allergic reaction, asthmatic attack, or seizure?
- Students don't make it to the meeting place on time?
- Someone gets separated from the group?

Making alternate plans in advance may save the event—it may even save lives.

Discussion Questions

1. When have you been surprised by a safety issue? How did you respond?

2. What safety assumptions do you tend to make about your various ministry programs?

3. What can you do to be better prepared for nearly every contingency?

For Further Study
• Meditate on Proverbs 20:18—"Plans are established by seeking advice; so if you wage war, obtain guidance." How does this passage relate to your ministry?

• Spend some time reflecting on Luke 17:2 and how Jesus' strong statement might apply to youth ministry safety.

Avoiding an Avoidable Mess
• Consider possible safety issues in each aspect of your ministry—games, activities, events, small groups, transportation, and so forth—and make adjustments where necessary.

• Make sure your staff is thoroughly briefed on what having a safe environment means.

CORRALLING CREEPS
Chapter 10 covered the "moral minefield," and that discussion relates directly to safety. Nothing can be more emotionally devastating for a young person than to be sexually abused. And allegations of sexual abuse will quickly destroy a ministry and ministry leader.

An unfortunate reality is that youth-serving organizations and churches will sometimes attract people who seek to prey on young people. We shouldn't assume that everyone who volunteers to work with young people has ulterior motives, of course. But we also shouldn't naively assume that someone is fine just because he's available and willing to serve.

We must keep the "creeps" from creeping into the ministry!

So you'll need an effective process for selecting your staff and volunteers. Jack Crabtree has much to say about this in *Better Safe Than Sued*, including steps to take and suggestions for a written application. The bottom line is that you need to carefully screen everyone who will be working with students: Sponsors, small group leaders, chaperones, mentors, camp counselors, drivers, coaches, teachers...*everyone*.

Jack writes:

Screening and background checks are now standard procedure with churches and youth organizations aware of the danger of sexual abusers and predators. These groups recognize their responsibility to protect the children and youth under their care. The screening process must be consistent, with an established standard of investigation for each level of leadership involvement. That standard should be applied equally, without discrimination, to every individual seeking to be involved in the ministry. Being a longtime member of the church, a church officer, or a friend of the pastor shouldn't exclude a person from the necessary review.

No process is foolproof. But every church and organization must take reasonable and consistent steps to obtain information that would reveal any past behavior that might predict potentially dangerous behavior by an employee or volunteer.

Keep the ministry safe by corralling the creeps.

Discussion Questions

1. How does someone join your ministry staff? What's the selection process?

2. Do you have a written application for potential volunteers? What information does the application request?

3. What should you do to improve this process?

For Further Study

• Even those who look and sound good can be rotten on the inside. Reflect on Jeremiah 17:9, John 3:19, and Romans 3:23—strong statements about every person's sin nature.

• Meditate on Ephesians 5:11 and consider what you might do to "expose" the "deeds of darkness."

Avoiding an Avoidable Mess

• Contact other churches and youth ministries and request copies of their staff application forms so you can improve yours.

• Ask a lawyer about what issues can be asked about on such forms and get advice on the right way to exclude someone about whom you have suspicions.

ON THE ROAD

I (Dave) was a junior in college and eager to drive home for spring break. So after my last class, I loaded my car (an old Pontiac sedan that drove like a tank) and picked up another student who'd be driving with me. Our destination was only 90 miles away—not too long a trip.

As I was pulling away from the dorm, I came to a stop sign. But the car wouldn't stop. I pumped the brakes furiously, and the pedal kept hitting the floor; but the car kept rolling—until I pulled the emergency brake. Now what? Since it was early evening, getting the brakes fixed would probably mean delaying our trip a day. And, hey, we had only 90 miles to drive...and the emergency brake worked. No big deal! So we decided to go for it.

Oh, and one other thing: A dense fog had rolled in. But that didn't stop us either, no way!

So that's what I did. I drove slowly on busy highways and tried to stay close behind another vehicle so I could see their taillights through the fog. (I couldn't see anything else.) And I used the emergency brake whenever I had to stop.

Either one of those conditions—no brakes or the thick fog—would make the driving conditions hazardous at best. The only sane decision would have been to wait and drive a safe car in safer conditions. But who said anything about being sane? We were college students—young and invincible!

I'm sure you're thinking, *What an idiot!* And you're right, of course. But similar scenarios play out all the time in youth ministry—with unsafe drivers manning unsafe vehicles in unsafe conditions—and often with tragic results.

Let's take a closer look at each of those factors.

Drivers

Transporting young people is a great burden. The parents of these precious children have entrusted them to our care. Therefore, we dare not turn them over to unqualified, immature, or careless drivers.

So here's a news flash: *No teenage drivers!* This means we should never allow high school students to transport their classmates in a ministry-sanctioned event or trip.

Obviously, students will drive friends to a meeting place, just as they'd drive other students to school, on a date, or to a show or concert. And after an event, the youth leader might suggest that everyone meet somewhere for pizza. But that's much different than a "sponsored" or "official" youth ministry activity—traveling to a camp or retreat, transporting kids to the airport for a mission trip, driving on the spring break adventure, and even organizing a caravan of cars going from the church to the big game.

Here are three more quick points about drivers:

1. All drivers should be responsible adults with valid driver's licenses. In Louisiana, the local Campus Life chapter held an annual "All-Night Whatchamacallit" where busloads of students would go from site to site and activity to activity (the mall, the ice skating rink, the bowling alley, the gym, and a restaurant for breakfast). One club was able to borrow a church bus for the event, but they needed a qualified driver. So the club director went to get his bus license. He was required to take a 50-question written test (no road test), and he needed a score of 80 percent to pass. (In other words, he could miss 10 questions.) On that test just five of the questions related specifically to driving a bus. He got all five of them wrong. But he passed the test and drove the kids. Hmmmm...? He was legal but not exactly qualified.

2. We need enough well-rested drivers with enough rest for the amount of driving required. On long trips many youth groups will drive all night. This cuts down on the potty breaks and traffic jams. But, obviously, it will lead to sleepy drivers. So in those situations, we need to have an alternate driver for each vehicle and plans for switching out and taking time to sleep.

3. Our drivers need to drive safely. Teenagers will urge the drivers to tailgate, swerve, honk, and so forth, especially toward other group vehicles. They'll also urge their driver to go faster and to pass and beat the other cars to the destination. As much as we all like young people and want to make them happy, we need to resist those temptations.

I (Len) remember one summer when I took two 15-passenger vans full of kids to the zoo. On the way back, my buddy (who was one of my interns) and I got into a "race" to see who could get back to the church first. I think he had the boys with him, and I had the girls with me. We didn't wreck or have any close calls, thank God, but we definitely were guilty of speeding, being stupid and reckless, and setting a terrible example for the students who were cheering and chanting, "Go, go, go!" "Faster!" "Don't let them beat us!" and other typical encouragements. And we did.

Come to think of it, that wasn't a good training moment for my intern either.

Vehicles

A safe vehicle is one in which everything works properly: The engine, transmission, lights, brakes(!), turn signals, heating and cooling system, mirrors, and window wipers. The tires need to be in good shape and properly inflated. And a seatbelt should be available and in good working order for every passenger.

We probably should also mention that the doors and locks should all work.

If you're planning to make a trip that will take more than an hour, then it's wise to have a mechanic give the vehicles a thorough inspection beforehand.

Conditions

As we've mentioned, teenagers will want to take risks, to "go for it." Certainly that includes driving in unsafe conditions like dense fog, thunderstorms, flooded highways, icy roads, blizzards or blowing snow, heavy winds, and others. This is where we must show our maturity and not take those chances, even if it means arriving late.

Bad weather doesn't always necessitate canceling the trip. Sometimes it means driving slower, taking different routes, or driving different vehicles. It means being wise.

We also shouldn't pack a vehicle with bodies. Either we plan well and have enough cars, vans, or buses (with a seat and seatbelt for each person), or we don't take everyone.

On the road again? Drive safely.

Discussion Questions
1. When have you compromised safety in driving?

2. If you could replay those experiences, what would you do differently?

For Further Study
• Read chapter 7 of Jack Crabtree's *Better Safe Than Sued*, called "Buses, Vans, and Automobiles."

Avoiding an Avoidable Mess
• Write a transportation policy and make sure everyone on your staff understands it.

• Be sure to notify the parents of this policy—they will greatly appreciate your efforts to keep them informed and to keep their children safe.

PERMISSION SLIPS AND RELEASE FORMS

"You did what?! If I'd known that's what you had in mind, I never would have given my permission!"

Many youth leaders have heard similar statements from frustrated or angry parents. Conventional wisdom says, "Getting forgiveness is easier than getting permission." Not with parents—and especially not when we're dealing with their children. Full disclosure is the only way to go. This means informing moms and dads about every aspect of the ministry, especially when risk and safety are involved.

One of the most important communication pieces is the permission slip. Some may dispute the legal value of these forms. After all, they say that if a church, organization, or any other entity is negligent, then the leaders are liable regardless of what was signed. Maybe. But don't get hung up on that. Instead, think honest communication—*full disclosure.*

Let's say, for example, that on a retreat you decide to offer rappelling—the exciting controlled fall (walk) by means of a harness and ropes—down the face of a cliff. For now, we'll assume that you used a skilled instructor and faultless equipment, that you took all the necessary safety precautions (no negligence here), and that everything worked out fine—everyone had a good time and no one got hurt. Now, how do you think the parents will react? A good bet is that several will be very upset that you put their son or daughter in a risky, life-endangering activity without asking for their permission. And if, God forbid, something terrible had happened, you'd have been toast.[5]

The best approach is to have parents fill out a specific *permission form* for each special activity. This form should describe the specific activity and dates for which the parents or guardian are granting permission for the student to participate.

As already mentioned, a signed release form doesn't protect a leader or group from being sued by a parent for negligence. No one can contract away negligence. But a signed release does prove that a parent or guardian gave permission for the student to be involved.

A major cause for lawsuits involving youth programs is surprise. Parents with little knowledge of the activities in which their children are participating are understandably upset when something goes wrong. Avoid this by providing parents with as much information as possible prior to the trip or event. You can verbally explain an activity at a pre-event meeting, but you should also put the information in writing and give it to the parents. Listing the risky activities and asking parents to initial their approval of their son or daughter's participation makes for a much-improved consent form.

5. By now you've probably gathered that we think reading *Better Safe Than Sued* is a good idea. That's true. In fact, most of the rest of this section has been adapted from chapter 16, specifically pages 208-211.

It's good to have parents sign a basic, generalized permission form that would cover most normal group-related activities. Keep a signed copy of this form on file and another copy with you. In addition, use specific consent forms for the following activities:

- An overnight trip—always
- A day trip to someplace outside of your area—always
- Any activity that's out of the ordinary—always

Check with a lawyer to work out the recommended wording for the forms. In addition, keep the lines of communication open with the parents of the young people involved in your program. More contact and communication mean fewer problems and the reduced chance of legal action.

Your commitment to safety and protection will be tested when a student arrives at the departure point for an overnight trip without her release or medical form. It would be very foolish to allow that person to go on the trip, despite the pressure you'll feel from yourself and the other students. Send a message to everyone in your group about keeping the standards. Years later, they'll thank you for standing strong.

Health and liability release forms are another valuable tool to protect everyone in the ministry and to provide the best care for students. In an emergency, a signed health form might make the difference between a student receiving immediate care and having to wait until a family member can be contacted. Having a complete medical history gives medical personnel the information that may speed their ability to make a correct diagnosis and treatment. Having complete factual information about students, their families, and their insurance assists you in completing the extensive information forms used in most hospitals. Leaders (counselors, chaperones, drivers, and others) should fill out these forms, too.

Health forms can be filled out annually and kept on file for students. But a parent's signature is still needed for each activity to confirm that the health information given previously is still current.

Most importantly, you must have immediate access to the forms whenever you need them. Work out a system that allows several people to know where the forms can be found. Keep the forms in a central location that can be easily accessed. You, as the leader, should keep a full set of forms for the group, but each volunteer leader should also have copies of the forms for the students riding in their car or staying in their cabin on a trip. If you were to be separated or have an accident, then everyone would have all the appropriate information.

Paperwork is a pain, and it may seem like more bureaucratic busy-work. But these forms can save everyone a lot of grief.

Discussion Questions

1. What questions do you think parents want answered about youth ministry events?

2. Why might a parent withhold permission for a son or daughter to be involved in a youth group activity?
3. For what events and activities do you normally use parent permission and liability release forms?

For Further Study

• Spend some time reflecting on what being a parent means and how you might feel if your son or daughter were injured during a youth ministry activity.

• Meditate on Matthew 7:12 (the Golden Rule) and think about how it applies to youth ministry safety issues.

Avoiding an Avoidable Mess

• Collect permission slips and release forms from churches and Christian organizations around town. Compare them and design your own.

• Get health forms from all your staff members.

TRIP DO'S AND DON'TS

Mark Oestreicher tells this story about his youth ministry nightmare (or, at least, "bad dream"):

> I'd always heard how I should take a head count when the kids piled into the van or bus—every time. And on big trips with lots of kids, I always did this. But I was sloppy on small trips with 10 or fewer kids. That is, until I lost a 13-year-old girl at night, in one of the most dangerous neighborhoods in downtown Chicago.
>
> We were on an inner-city mission trip. Late in the evening, on our way back to the semi-abandoned but secure apartment building that was our home away from home, we stopped for a snack at McDonald's. I'd looked around to see if anyone was still in the restaurant when we were leaving, but I hadn't counted or checked the names of our students. When we left, Laura was in the restroom.

She waited at the restaurant for a half-hour, hoping I'd realize she was missing and come back for her. When that didn't happen and since she knew the way, she proceeded on a five-block walk of terror. Gang members shouted obscenities and threats at her. And when she finally got to our building, the door was locked, and we were safely sheltered on the third floor.

I will never forget the feelings of total failure, panic, and thankfulness I felt when one of the students came running into my room to tell me Laura was pounding on the outside door. I still hadn't realized she was missing!

The moral of Marko's story? When traveling with a group, make sure you do a headcount when boarding buses, vans, or cars *every time*. Here are some other trip do's and don'ts to help you avoid your own horror story.

DO'S
- Have a good staff-to-student ratio (no more than 1 to 10).
- If possible, have a health professional on your trip: Doctor, nurse, or veterinarian. (Just kidding!)
- A few days before leaving, double-check all travel plans: Routes, stops, reservations, hours of operation, and other important details.
- Beforehand, design a phone tree for communicating to all the parents. This is especially helpful in an emergency or when arrival times change drastically.
- Before leaving, have a brief parents' meeting during which you reiterate the travel itinerary, trip rules, and phone tree.
- Pray with parents, leaders, and students before boarding buses, vans, or cars.
- Have a travel plan, including dinner and rest stops, and make sure every staff person has a copy of the plan, as well as directions (a map).
- Make contingency plans.
- Be sure everyone has a seatbelt.
- If you hire a bus company, then let the professionals do their job.
- With more than one vehicle, be sure vehicle leaders can communicate with one another.
- Make sure your designated staff person has all the medical release and history forms.
- Equip a staff person in each vehicle with snacks and possible games or songs to help pass the time.
- Call ahead to eating establishments to let them know you'll be stopping there for a meal—so they can be ready.
- Keep the group together when you stop.
- Make your meal, restroom, and fuel stops in known, safe areas.

- Enforce the rules.
- Know the location of the vehicle's safety and first-aid kits.

DON'TS
- If you hire a bus company, don't assume the drivers know the directions to your destination—double-check everything with them.
- Don't sacrifice safety for timing or convenience.
- Don't allow students (or staff) to talk you into doing something you shouldn't.
- Don't allow anything to hang out the windows, including trash, hands, or feet.
- Don't take chances while driving.
- Don't expect 100 teenagers to finish eating in a half-hour at one establishment.
- Don't tolerate any use of alcohol, drugs, or tobacco.
- Don't store luggage where it might fall on someone.
- Don't clutter the vehicle's aisle or exit.
- Don't lose any vehicle in the caravan—know where they all are.
- Don't take a shortcut unless you've gone that way before.

You probably can add to these lists. Just remember: Safety first!

Discussion Questions
1. What do you find most useful when planning your trip route: An Internet service like MapQuest or a GPS? Why? How can you use the strengths of both?

2. What safety issue concerns you the most on trips?

3. What can you do to make sure you leave and return on time?

For Further Study
- Spend some time reflecting on Romans 8:38-39. Consider how the promise that we can never be lost to God and his love relates to youth ministry events, especially trips.

Avoiding an Avoidable Mess
- Make your own checklist of trip do's and don'ts and circulate it among your staff.

GETTING BETTER

I (Len) walked out to get the mail the other day, and there, nestled in the stack of bills and junk mail, was a letter from the American Association of Retired People (AARP). Since then, my teenage sons have been mocking me mercilessly.

Even though (as I type this sentence) I won't turn 50 for 50 more days, some stranger in an office somewhere found out about my milestone birthday. She (this *had* to be a "she" because no "he" is that organized or thoughtful) then notified another group of kindly souls who immediately created an AARP card with my name on it.

The card sits on my kitchen counter, plastic documentation of the fact that, having graduated from childhood, survived adolescence, and zoomed through adulthood, I have now officially arrived at geezerdom.

Turning 50 has its up side—discounts on reading glasses and reduced prices at the all-you-can-eat buffet up the street. But it also means it's time for my comprehensive medical checkup.

I don't want to do it. A battery of intensely personal questions. Lots of bare skin on a very cold, steel exam table. Being poked and prodded. Vampires disguised in white lab coats. Little plastic cups. Tiny cameras in unthinkable places.

A thorough medical evaluation like that isn't pleasant, but it is necessary. The point is to assess, to take a comprehensive look and search for signs of trouble—and if any problems exist, to deal with them in order to keep minor issues from becoming major deals.

Guess what? It's not just a *medical* exam that's a good idea. Personal *spiritual* and *professional* evaluation is also important. And not just when you're on the verge of turning 50.

If I knew then what I know now, I'd have made sure that I incorporated regular job performance checkups. Without them, there's no way to get better.

THE IMPORTANCE OF PERSONAL EVALUATION

In the quarter-century I (Len) have spent in full-time vocational ministry, I've had no more than *seven* official job evaluations. In my 10-plus years of working full time with students, my bosses sat me down for a performance review twice—maybe.

Don't get me wrong. I don't relish meeting with superiors and hearing where I've fallen short. I'm not clamoring to replay my failures or revisit unaccomplished goals. But I also know (in my better, braver, saner moments) that without regular, objective appraisals of my ministry performance, I can't very well improve.

Question: Why do we resist an exercise that has so much potential to enhance our lives and increase our effectiveness? When it comes to personal evaluation, consider three truths:

- **Scripture commands it.** Jeremiah urged his countrymen: "Let us examine our ways and test them, and let us return to the Lord" (Lamentations 3:40). Paul instructed the church at Corinth: "Examine yourselves to see whether you are in the faith; test yourselves (2 Corinthians 13:5).
- **Common sense requires it.** Socrates declared, "The unexamined life is not worth living." Sigmund Freud added, "Being entirely honest with oneself is a good exercise."
- **God is able to help us in the process.** Jeremiah addressed the Lord as "you who examine the righteous and probe the heart and mind" (Jeremiah 20:12). And David prayed: "Search me, God, and know my heart; test me and know my anxious thoughts. See if there is any offensive way in me, and lead me in the way everlasting" (Psalm 139:23-24).

I was young and working in a large suburban congregation (about 2,000 in worship). One of my first youth ministry events drew nearly 600 young people, so naturally I was pretty excited. And the pastor gave me all kinds of "attaboys" because of the large turnout. Soon a pattern emerged— he'd be profuse in his praise when attendance was good but not so much at other times. He always encouraged me to get more and more young people involved in Sunday school, youth group, youth retreats, youth camp, and other youth events. For him, attendance was everything, the sole criterion for success. I wasn't encouraged to look at more spiritual indicators, such as households of faith. Through the years, I've learned that a much better indicator of ministry effectiveness is the number of homes or families that have been equipped to live for Jesus, rather than numbers of youth being drawn to the "God-building."
—*David Lynn*

Medical experts keep telling us that many life-threatening diseases are curable if diagnosed early and treated aggressively. The problem is, far too many people *never* even get a checkup. Out of fear that doctors *might* find something wrong, they resist routine medical exams. It's only a matter of time before doctors discover grave problems, and by then the prognosis is grim.

Don't make a similar mistake with your youth ministry. Seek out evaluations and submit to them. Listen. Ponder. Ask for help. Determine to make corrections and get better.

Discussion Questions

1. What's your experience (and your honest feelings) with regard to job evaluations?

2. When someone points out your failings, do you get (a) defensive, (b) nervous, (c) angry, (d) discouraged, (e) motivated, or (f) other?

3. What's the difference between criticism and *constructive* criticism?

4. What would you say to a person who received a less-than-positive performance evaluation? How could that individual avoid going in the tank emotionally and feeling like a loser?

For Further Study

• Look up the following Proverbs and consider what each has to say about the benefit of hearing and accepting constructive criticism: Proverbs 9:9; 12:15; 13:10; 13:13; 15:32; and 17:10.

• Ponder deeply this stunning statement of David in Psalm 141:5—"Let a righteous man strike me—that is a kindness; let him rebuke me—it is oil on my head. My head will not refuse it."

Avoiding an Avoidable Mess

• Ask your colleagues these questions: What's it like to work with me? How am I doing? What do I do that annoys you?

• Find out from your boss or supervisor what your church or ministry's policies are on job reviews. When do they occur? Who participates? On what basis are employees evaluated?

• If, for some strange reason, your bosses resist giving you official feedback, get feedback from your students, their parents, and your volunteers. Ask for their opinions. Give them surveys. Encourage them to shoot straight—about the job you're doing.

• When you receive a job review, don't bury it in a file and flush it from your mind. Pick at least three areas of weakness and, with your boss, come up with a workable plan for addressing these issues.

A LEADER IS A READER

Once again I (Len) am dating myself here, but when I became a full-time youth minister in 1980, cable TV was just beginning to go mainstream. Over a two- to three-year stretch, my roommates and I became addicts of an upstart all-news channel called CNN. We watched mind-blowing music videos on another new channel called MTV (back when that network actually showed music videos). We shook our heads at a network called ESPN that had the audacious goal of broadcasting sports 24 hours a day. (One day, after trying to understand an Australian Rules Football telecast, I shook my head and flatly declared, "ESPN will *never* survive.")

But even if I didn't see a future in televised cricket and curling, I still had 20 other channels to choose from. (This was jaw-dropping since I grew up with just *four* channels: ABC, NBC, CBS, and PBS.) The bottom line: I spent *lots* of my downtime just clicking away with the remote.

If I knew then what I know now, I would have turned off the tube and picked up more books. And more than just picking them up (or stacking them by my bedside), I would have actually read them.

A colleague in ministry always used to tell his kids: "Remember, a reader is a leader, and a leader is a reader." How true that is—a bit cheesy, perhaps, but true nonetheless.

As a wet-behind-the-ears, fresh-out-of-college youth worker, I read some but not nearly enough. Looking back, I'd gladly trade all those

A HANDFUL OF CLASSICS EVERY YOUTH PASTOR SHOULD READ

Celebration of Discipline by Richard J. Foster

Disappointment with God by Philip Yancey

Mere Christianity by C. S. Lewis

The Practice of the Presence of God by Brother Lawrence

The Pursuit of God by A. W. Tozer

The Pursuit of Holiness by Jerry Bridges

The Supremacy of God in Preaching by John Piper

hours wasted watching the Chicago Cubs on WGN and the Atlanta Braves on TBS for a little more usable knowledge.

Here are a few practical thoughts on reading:

- Develop a reading plan and set some concrete goals. Even if you're not a speed-reader, if you devote at least 30 minutes a day to reading, it's usually possible to read two books a month. Pick out 24 books you want to tackle over the next year. Go ahead. Make a list. Then visit the library (or book-store) and start turning pages.
- Choose a wide variety of reading material. In any given year, stretch your mind by digesting at least a couple of works of quality *fiction* (perhaps one classic and one recent). Include a work of *theology*, a *biography* or two, something *devotional*, something *historical*, and at least one social sciences book on *cultural trends*. Obviously, you'll want to choose a couple of *professional development* books (such as a book on becoming a better speaker), a title on *leadership*, and a couple of books *specific to youth ministry*.
- If you have an author that you've always wanted to check out—you might decide to declare the next 12 months, for example, "My C. S. Lewis Reading Year."
- Ask an older Christian leader or admired spiritual mentor what books have impacted him or her the most.
- Try to read at whatever time your brain is most awake and alert. (If you're one of those fortunate souls who fall asleep within 30 seconds of your head hitting the pillow, then bedtime is *not* your optimal reading time.)
- Have lively conversations with the author as you read. Not literally, but write in your books. (Unless, of course, it's a borrowed book.) Underline. Highlight. Jot down questions or objections in the margins. I promise

the Library of Congress police won't arrest you. If you just can't bring yourself to defile the printed page, at least use sticky notes to mark great quotes or helpful passages.
- If, at the end of the first year of your new "lifetime reading experiment," you discover that you didn't read your 24 chosen books—not even 12 of them, but only six—then hey, that's still a half-dozen books you might not have read otherwise.

Discussion Questions

1. What are your current reading habits? If you are an avid reader, what sparked your interest in books? If not, why do you think that is?

2. What books have impacted you the most deeply and why?

3. What books are you hearing great buzz about that you'd like to read?

4. What are some subjects you'd like to learn more about?

5. How well do you typically remember what you've read?

For Further Study

• Notice how Apollos is described in Acts 18:24-25. Can a person be considered "learned" without a serious reading habit?

• What do you think Ecclesiastes 12:12 means?

• Second Timothy is the last letter Paul ever wrote. Notice what the apostle asked for in the final paragraphs (4:13).

Avoiding an Avoidable Mess

• Always take a book wherever you go. So much of life involves waiting around—for meetings, for events to start, for doctor appointments, for flights, and so on. You never know when you're going to have a half-hour with nothing to do.

• Join a book discussion club or form your own. There's nothing like a little monthly accountability to help acquire and cultivate the all-important reading habit. A stimulating conversation with some good thinkers can help you ferret out a good takeaway or two from each book you read.

• Put books on your Amazon Wish List; let supportive parents and family members know that for birthdays, Christmas, or Clergy Appreciation month, you'd really love to get some good reading material. Put the word out that gift cards to LifeWay or Barnes and Noble are desirable, too.

MENTORS

On paper the idea of mentoring looks great—an older, wiser Christian taking you under his wing and offering guidance, wisdom, and encouragement. Who wouldn't love to have that?

If you already have such a person in your life, fall on your knees and thank the Lord. Take advantage of this rare blessing. Revel in it. Soak up everything you possibly can. Ask a million questions. Take notes.

If you don't have a mentor, pray about that. Ask God to bring a sage person into your life who can teach you valuable life lessons and pass on God-honoring skills. Potential mentors can be found in your church or ministry organization. Consider, for example, elders and other church officers, parents of former youth group participants, and ministry board members and spouses. Ask your pastor for suggestions.

Many young people report that despite fervent prayer and searching, actually finding a flesh-and-blood mentor is a difficult proposition. I have some theories on why this is so.

More and more, churches segregate the generations. Teenagers tend to remain aloof in their own little youth bubble. Senior adults congregate in their Sunday school classes and the local cafeteria. Twenty-somethings hang out together at Starbucks.

Also, many churches have multiple services. You might attend the same church for five years and never even *meet* many of your fellow church members.

Add to that the fact that most folks are already overcommitted in their personal lives and the reality that so many people relocate every three to four years and, well, let's be honest: Mentoring—for millions of people—is only a nice theory, a mere wish-dream.

For sure, nothing beats a flesh-and-blood mentor. So don't give up trying to find one. But until God brings that person across your path, here's an idea to consider: *A mentor from the past.*

Think of all those renowned saints from church history—great thinkers and leaders like Augustine, Martin Luther, John Bunyan, Charles Spurgeon, C. S. Lewis, Catherine Marshall, Rosalind Rinker, A. W. Tozer, or Mother Teresa. Even though they're all in heaven now, these men and women remain accessible through their writings! We can spend time at their feet, gleaning from their rich experiences and letting their faith inspire us to a deeper walk with God.

Here's an example of how a person might be "mentored" by C. S. Lewis for an entire year (in just a few minutes a day):

- Begin by reading his short autobiography, *Surprised by Joy*, which tells of his childhood and his conversion to Christ (estimated reading time: one month).
- Spend two months thinking your way through Lewis' masterwork *Mere Christianity* (33 chapters), in which he makes a brilliant case for the reasonableness of the Christian faith.
- Take a month to tackle *Miracles*.
- Take four months to read his best-selling Chronicles of Narnia, a seven-volume, easy and fun-to-read fantasy-adventure series filled with numerous allusions to the gospel.
- Take a month to read and reflect on the often hilarious and always thought-provoking *The Screwtape Letters*—an imaginative look at how the Devil and his demons work.
- If you've stayed on schedule, you'll have three months left. Don't miss the chance to spend at least half of that time exposing your mind and heart to *The Great Divorce*, an imaginative and thought-provoking bus ride from hell to heaven.
- Finish your year with Lewis with the short volume *A Grief Observed*. He penned this poignant memoir after the death of his wife. It's a raw and honest telling of despair, doubt, and restored faith.

You could take a similar approach with any great leader from the past. Having trouble finding a flesh-and-blood mentor? Look in your library!

Discussion Questions

1. Up to this point in your life, what people has God used most significantly to shape you?

2. What qualities would you look for in a mentor? Why?

3. Look around your church. Is there *anyone* who's a bit more "seasoned" who might also be a potential mentor? What about an older minister at another church?

4. What are the necessary ingredients for a successful mentoring relationship?

5. Who are the people in your life *right now* who are pouring into you— who teach you, challenge you, and hold you accountable?

For Further Study

• Spend some time reflecting on the relationship between the great leader Moses and his young protégé Joshua. (See Exodus 24:13; 33:11; Numbers 11:28; 27:18-22; and Deuteronomy 1:38.)

• Read Paul's two letters to Timothy. What terrific counsel from a mentor to a younger believer!

Avoiding an Avoidable Mess

• Take your list from question three above and start making phone calls.

• Even if you haven't found an older and wiser mentor, you can at least form an accountability group. Find one or two peers and meet with them regularly. Ask each other tough questions. Agree to be transparent and authentic with one another. Make it your goal to encourage each other and "spur one another on toward love and good deeds" (Hebrews 10:24).

PROFESSIONAL DEVELOPMENT

Like millions of others, I (Len) sat mesmerized in a darkened theater back in 1981, with members of my youth group clustered all around me as we watched actor Harrison Ford play an adventuresome archaeologist named Indiana Jones.

Ford perfectly summed up my youth ministry experience in one memorable exchange from *Raiders of the Lost Ark*:

Indy: I gotta get on that truck.

Sallah: How?

Indy: *(mumbling)* I don't know; I'm making this up as I go.

"I'm making this up as I go." That was my life as a novice youth worker.

With so many things flying at me—students' needs, parents' requests, personal responsibilities—and so many variables changing all the time, taking care of what was in front of me in the moment was tough enough, much less finding the time to think ahead and work at getting better at the task of ministry.

Yet, if youth ministers don't intentionally and strategically work on improving, the law of entropy will gradually cause them to stagnate or even regress.

If you feel clueless about lots of things, understand this: You're in touch with reality! There's a *ton* you don't know—including a lot of stuff you'll *never* master this side of heaven.

And if you feel incompetent in certain areas, know also that you're in good company. Every honest youth minister—heck, every minister period—feels inadequate. Only an egomaniac with major denial issues says, "I can't possibly learn more or get better at my job."

How can a busy youth worker who's "making it up as she goes" get better at ministry? Consider these practical suggestions:

- Take an online class. Most Bible colleges and seminaries offer basic courses in theology or Bible exposition. Perhaps your church or ministry would even be willing to help subsidize the cost.
- Check out the continuing education courses at a nearby university or community college. Schools often advertise evening courses on a wide array of subjects—computers, software training, photography, basic Greek, public speaking, guitar, event management, and so on. I even took a night course in juggling. (I can't pay the bills with that skill, but it's a good trick to have in the bag.)
- As we've already mentioned, become a voracious reader (especially in those subjects where you're weak).
- Find the parent in your group who's a good mechanic. When your car breaks down, see if he will help you out (while you watch). You never know when a little basic mechanical know-how might salvage a youth trip gone awry.
- Subscribe to a couple of good professional publications. *YouthWorker Journal* is one of the best (www.youthworker.com). *Group* is also a great source.
- Go to conferences. Do everything possible to get to the National Youth Workers Convention. Submit a budget request. Save your shekels. Sell your blood. Youth Specialties usually sponsors two or three around the country each year. (Visit www.nywc.com for more details.) If you can't swing the big enchilada, then at least try to attend a couple of smaller one- or two-day workshops (www.ysoneday.com).
- Watch the History Channel. Doing so deepens your knowledge and gives you a deeper "well" to draw from.

And again, remember that increased ministry effectiveness is not simply a function of acquiring more knowledge or skills. Living out the command to "excel still more" (1 Thessalonians 4:1 and 10 NASB) requires us to take care of our hearts.

Some quick reminders:

- Get a life (outside of being a youth minister). All work and no play makes Jack (or Jacqueline) a really dull person.
- Get away. Travel every chance you get. If you have cash flow issues, go to the local park, the municipal golf course, the public library, a friend's lake house, or an out-of-the-way coffee shop.

- Take a day. Enjoy the silence. (And give your computer and cell phone a sabbath rest, too—no texting, emailing, or Internet.)
- Join a good small group.
- Find and enjoy a hobby. Not an expensive or exhausting one, but a replenishing one.
- Figure out what your "therapy" is. My wife's is relaxing by our fireplace. I actually enjoy splitting firewood (which works out well!). I know one minister's wife who plays the piano to unwind. When she's done, she feels refreshed and ready to engage. It makes her better, more effective.
- Join a gym. Get in shape and keep yourself in good physical condition. A great spirit trapped in a wrecked body isn't much good to anyone.
- Take care of yourself (adequate sleep, eating right). You've only got one life. Doesn't it make sense to take care of it?

Discussion Questions

1. What was the deal with that dreadful *Indiana Jones and the Temple of Doom* movie? Has there ever been a worse sequel to a great movie?

2. In what areas of your life or ministry have you made major, positive strides? How did you do it?

3. What's a skill you wish you had? Is there a reasonable way for you to develop this ability?

4. In what specific areas of ministry would you like to improve?

5. How can a youth minister guard against complacency?

For Further Study

• Galatians 5:25 tells us to "keep in step with the Spirit." It's a good reminder that the Christian life is a walk, a journey. We're moving, following, letting God lead. We cannot afford to get stagnant or ·stop growing.

• The writer of Hebrews repeatedly used the word *better* (Hebrews 6:9; 7:19, 22; 8:6; 9:23; 10:34; 11:4, 16, 35, 40; 12:24). Why did he do this, do you think?

• Memorize 2 Peter 3:18—"But grow in the grace and knowledge of our Lord and Savior Jesus Christ. To him be glory both now and forever! Amen."

Avoiding an Avoidable Mess

• Have someone videotape you the next time you speak to your group. Force yourself to watch it. You'll see what your audience sees— the good stuff, as well as the annoying mannerisms. It's the only way to get better.

• Remember, the more skills you have, the more you can offer your employer and the more marketable and valuable you become.

• Don't just settle for a bunch of vague thoughts of what you "could do" or all the obscure ways you'd like to "get better." Make a concrete three-month plan. Make it reasonable, achievable, and measurable. Show it to a couple of friends or colleagues. Ask them to hold you accountable.

ASSESSING YOUR OVERALL MINISTRY

As we mentioned at the beginning of this book, the two of us (Dave and Len) have spent a total of nearly 60 years in youth ministry. That's so many young friends over the years, so many faces from the past. We've lost touch with most of the people we worked with during their teenage years. We sometimes wonder how their lives have unfolded. How did they turn out? Where are they now?

Thanks to the Internet, email, Facebook, and so forth, I (Len) have been able to reconnect with a few of them. And through their comprehensive social networks, I've been pleased to discover that some of the young people who passed through our group have weathered life's storms and are still walking with God. Sadly, I've also learned that many others have left the church.

Here's a reality: In youth ministry, we don't always get to see results. I believe you need three to five years to begin to see significant, long-term results—and you may never see them this side of eternity. That's one of the reasons we keep hearing that the average youth minister lasts only 18 months in the job. If it weren't for a few dinosaurs like me throwing off the curve, it would be even shorter. That's a shame—too many of us leave before we get to the good times.

—*Kent Keller*

A few students from my groups went on to great success—winning Grammys in Nashville, writing successful movie screenplays in Hollywood, scoring touchdowns in the NFL. Some married and raised happy families. But a bunch of others married with great hopes and promptly divorced. A handful have come out of the closet (one is a very famous gay activist—if I said her name, you'd probably know her). Many have battled (or still do) alcohol or drug addictions. A handful are no longer living (drug overdoses, or, in the sad case of one young man, killed along with his infant son in a senseless shootout with law enforcement officials).

I hear the tragic stories and the not-always-encouraging updates, I think about all those Bible lessons and counseling sessions and all that time I logged with youth. Years later, I see so much personal devastation and pain. And I wonder: *Did I make any difference at all?*

How do we measure success in ministry?

Faithfulness.

That's the only measuring stick I know.

We can't control teenagers—whether they really listen, what they do with the gospel, how they'll decide to live. We don't control them when they're under our care, much less when they're launched out into the world.

The only thing we can control (and then, only with God's help) is our own actions. So we keep putting it out there—God's truth. We lay our hearts—our lives down. We invest time and effort. We teach and encourage and exhort. And then we pray like there's no tomorrow. We cry out to God to please take our meager "widow's mite" of ministry and bless it and use it.

Faithfulness is what we contribute. Fruitfulness is God's work. Submission and obedience are our parts; results are God's department.

And more times than not, the results are hidden. In this life we seldom get to see the impact we've had.

Can you be okay with that reality? Trust us, you *need* to get okay with it because that's how things work.

But every now and then, you will get these little blessings, sweet confirmations that all was not in vain. Here's one example. I (Len) had this guy in my ministry in the early '90s. He was good-looking and very athletic. He fancied himself a player with the ladies, and—not surprisingly—he was quite full of himself. I didn't much enjoy him. Truth be told, I sort of endured him.

His life went the way of so many. He graduated and moved away, married young, and also married badly. They had kids right away. Like the saying goes, they were "kids having kids." Then his child bride up and left him. She didn't want to be married anymore. And while this young man was still reeling from the shock of a failed marriage and trying to work and raise two sons by himself, he developed some mysterious and debilitating health issues.

Each report got worse and worse until someone said he'd turned a corner. He'd remarried, but this time to a sweet Christian girl. I heard he was engaged with God again and plugged in at his church—*working with youth.*

Amazing, I thought.

Then one day he showed up at my office. He said he was just passing through town. This man was humble and sweet. He really was changed. He talked about a day—a day I don't even remember now—when I'd spent several hours with him, showing him some things, talking with him about some issues.

He'd come by, he said, just to see me and tell me how much he appreciated my ministry to him.

I went home that day with a smile. And each time I remember stories like that I smile again.

I (Dave) would sum up my own experience in a very similar way. I wish I knew then that my ministry was actually making a huge difference in so many lives. I remember walking on campus—in the cafeteria, down the halls, outside the gym at the trophy case, at the bus stop, or out on the field—and feeling as though I'd walked into a party where I hadn't been invited. Feeling psyched out and insecure and knowing few students, I often wondered what I was doing there. Looking back, however, I can see that those countless hours spent immersed in the adolescent world paid off. I knew God had called me to those campuses, but I sure had my doubts at the time, especially when kids seemed to be ignoring me and few were attending my meetings. Now, however, I see former "club kids" from broken or alcoholic or in other ways dysfunctional homes who are now mature parents (even grandparents) who are living for Christ, their lives having been transformed through the gospel.

I am humbled when I reconnect with these former high school and junior high school students who thank me for my part in the process. God used me despite my failings and lack of faith. God was at work, even when I didn't feel like it or see the evidence.

Discussion Questions

1. How would you define *faithfulness*?

2. When have you had someone thank you for your ministry investment in her life? What was that experience like?

3. In what specific areas of ministry do you find it most difficult to be faithful?

4. Imagine sitting at your own funeral and listening to your former youth group members talk about your life and your impact. What sorts of things would you want to hear them say?

For Further Study

• Spend some time reflecting on this phrase from 2 Corinthians 5:9— "So we make it our goal to please him." In what way does this mindset ensure ministry effectiveness?

• Check out Numbers 12:7.

• Ponder 2 Chronicles 31:20.

• Memorize Matthew 25:23.

Avoiding an Avoidable Mess

• Remember that you're only one factor in a student's life. Teenagers have parents or stepparents, peers, teachers, coaches, friends, and classmates—plus tons of media influence in their lives. If you blame yourself for every student who wrecks his life, then are you going to take full credit for every student who turns out "well"?

• Read the Aesop's Fable of "The Tortoise and the Hare." (Google it.) It's a short and powerful reminder that life is a marathon, not a sprint, and that the victor is the one who faithfully and consistently keeps plodding away.

ABOUT THE AUTHORS

Len Woods

For much of his adult life, Len Woods has been involved in student ministry. He's been a wild-eyed summer intern, a clueless part-time youth director, and a mistake-making full-time student pastor. He's been a bumbling adult volunteer, as well as a stumbling father of teenaged sons. The former editor of *Youthwalk*—a monthly devotional magazine for teens—Len has also authored and helped create numerous books and Bible study materials for youth and youth leaders.

Since Len can't have a do-over, *If I Knew Then…* is his hopeful attempt to help new youth workers learn from his own failures and the common—but avoidable—blunders of other student ministry veterans.

A graduate of LSU and Dallas Theological Seminary, Len is now the lead pastor at Christ Community Church in Ruston, Louisiana, (www. cccruston.com) where he still goofs up on a regular basis.

Dave Veerman

Dave, a graduate of Wheaton College and Trinity Evangelical Divinity School, worked for 26 years with Youth for Christ. He's authored more than 60 books, including *101 Questions Children Ask about God, Youth Evangelism, Reaching Out to Troubled Youth, Tough Parents for Tough Times, Understanding Your Teenager, When Your Father Dies,* and *Dave's Complete Guide to Junior High Ministry*. He served as a senior editor of the *Life Application Study Bible* and as the senior editor of the *Student Life Application Bible*.

Dave is also a founding partner in The Livingstone Corporation, a company that serves Bible publishers by creating, developing, and producing Bible-related products (www.livingstonecorp.com). In addition, he presents "Understanding Your Teenager" seminars across the country. Dave and his wife, Gail, have two grown daughters, are the proud grandparents of three granddaughters, and live in Naperville, Illinois.

Dave has been known to play his nose in venues across the world.

CONTRIBUTORS

J. T. Bean
Pastor of Congregational Life, First Evangelical Free Church
Rockford, Illinois
www.firstfreerockford.org

Les Christie
Chairman, Youth Ministry Department, William Jessup University
Rocklin, California
www.jessup.edu

Nate Conrad
Associate Pastor, Naperville Presbyterian Church
Naperville, Illinois
www.npchurch.org

Dave Corlew
Senior Pastor, Arlington Countryside Church
Arlington Heights, Illinois
www.acchurch.org

Jack Crabtree
Executive Director, Long Island Youth for Christ
Huntington Station, New York
www.liyfc.org

Jeff Dye
Minister to Students, Northcliffe Baptist Church
Spring Hill, Florida
www.northcliffeonline.org

Jim Green
Parenting Seminar Presenter, HomeWord
Auburn, Alabama
www.homeword.com

Rob Hankins
Area Director, Young Life
Naperville, Illinois
www.younglife.org

Bill Jackson
President, Radical Life Ministries
Corona, California
www.nothinsgonnastopit.com

Alan Johnson
Director of Wesley Foundation, University of Louisiana Monroe
Monroe, Louisiana
http://la-umc.org/campus.php

Kent Keller
Senior Pastor, Kendall Presbyterian Church
Miami, Florida
www.kendallpres.org

Chris Larsen
Pastor of Spiritual Development, Lake Hills Church
Austin, Texas
http://soulthirstcafe.com

David Lynn
Author and trainer
Tucson, Arizona
Learn about David's latest project at www.BringingFaithHomeonline.com.

Greg Monaco
National Field Associate, Youth for Christ
Lake in the Hills, Illinois
www.yfc.org

Tom Morris
Executive Director, YFC GrievingTeens
Palm Desert, California
www.yfcgrievingteens.org

Mark Oestreicher[6]
President, Youth Specialties
El Cajon, California
www.youthspecialties.com

6. All quotations from Marko originally appeared in articles on the Youth Specialties Web site (www.youthspecialties.com).

John O'Leary
Community Life Pastor, Fellowship Bible Church
Cabot, Arkansas
www.fbclr.org

Christopher Ribaudo
Founder and Creative Strategist, Ribaudo Associates
Wheaton, Illinois
www.ribaudoassociates.com

Todd Smith
Youth Minister, First Baptist Church
Tallahassee, Florida
www.fbctlh.org

Priscilla Steinmetz
Founder, The Bridge Teen Center
Tinley Park, Illinois
www.thebridgeteencenter.org

Matt Tucker
Youth Pastor, Woodburn Missionary Church
Woodburn, Indiana
www.woodburnmc.org

Paul Veerman
Regional Advisor, American Bible Society
New York, New York
www.americanbible.org

Dave Wager
President, Silver Birch Ranch
White Lake, Wisconsin
www.silverbirchranch.org

Neil Wilson
Senior Project Manager and author, The Livingstone Corporation
Carol Stream, Illinois
www.livingstonecorp.com